Wikipatterns

Wikipatterns

Stewart Mader

Wiley Publishing, Inc.

Wikipatterns

Published by
Wiley Publishing, Inc.
10475 Crosspoint Boulevard
Indianapolis, IN 46256
www.wiley.com

Copyright © 2008 by Wiley Publishing, Inc., Indianapolis, Indiana
Published simultaneously in Canada

ISBN: 978-0-470-22362-8

Manufactured in the United States of America

10 9 8 7 6 5 4 3 2 1

To Amy

It is not the strongest of the species that survives, nor the most intelligent, but those most adaptive to change.

Charles Darwin

About the Author

Stewart Mader is Wiki Evangelist for Atlassian Software Systems, and a noted wiki/social software researcher, author, blogger, and speaker. Before joining Atlassian, he worked with several universities and a number of other organizations to introduce wikis and grow wiki collaboration across departments, teams, and projects.

In 2007 he launched `Wikipatterns.com`, a community-built, wiki-based resource for people to share patterns and strategies for increasing wiki collaboration.

He also publishes Blog on Wiki Patterns (ikiw.org), which is his personal perspective on the uses and benefits of wiki collaboration.

In October 2006, he published *Using Wiki in Education* (wikiineducation.com), a book containing 10 wide-ranging case studies from teachers using the wiki to transform teaching and engage today's students. This is the first book to focus specifically on the wiki in education and be developed and published using a wiki, so it actively demonstrates the tool in action.

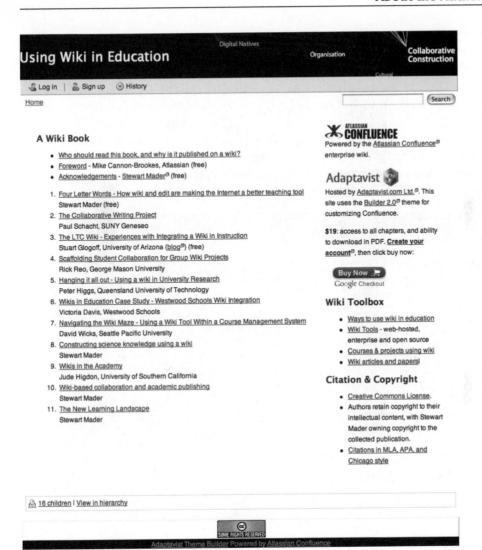

He has taught science both in the classroom and online, worked extensively with social software and wiki technology in education, and has worked with faculty to apply and assess its impact on student learning. He previously served as Senior Instructional Technologist for Life Sciences and Brown Medical School at Brown University, Educational Technologist at Emerson College, Instructional Designer and Interim Director of the Faculty Center for Learning Development at University of Hartford, and has collaborated with faculty at Long Island University on a series of teaching and learning projects.

He is cofounder of The Science of Spectroscopy (`scienceofspectroscopy.info`), a project that rethinks how spectroscopy is taught by using a model that starts with real-world applications, gets students engaged and asking "how does it work?" and then teaches techniques and theory. The website is wiki-based, making it easy for users to quickly edit pages and contribute information using just a web browser. The project has been featured in the journals *Science* and *Chemistry International*, is a member of the National Science Digital Library and the National Grid for Learning, and was recently named a member of 33 wikis, a showcase of the best in wiki-based collaboration.

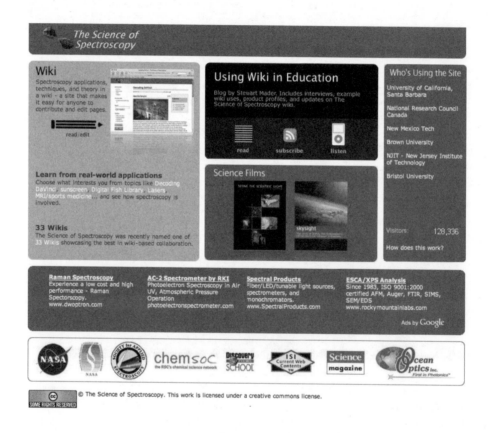

He has produced two films in collaboration with NASA. *Seeing the Scientific Light* and *Skysight* let students hear directly from scientists who use spectroscopy in their everyday work. The films have aired on PBS stations and are currently in retail distribution. He holds a B.S. in Chemistry from University of Hartford, and is pursuing an M.S. in Curriculum Development and Instructional Technology from University at Albany.

Credits

Executive Editor
Chris Webb

Development Editor
Adaobi Obi Tulton

Production Editor
Dassi Zeidel

Copy Editor
Mildred Sanchez

Editorial Manager
Mary Beth Wakefield

Production Manager
Tim Tate

Vice President and Executive Group Publisher
Richard Swadley

Vice President and Executive Publisher
Joseph B. Wikert

Project Coordinator, Cover
Lynsey Osborn

Proofreader
Jen Larsen, Word One

Indexer
Robert Swanson

Anniversary Logo Design
Richard Pacifico

Cover Image
©iStockphoto.com/Arthur Kwiatkowski

Contents at a Glance

Contents

Foreword

I launched the first wiki in March of 1995. I was an activist in a community of activists. We were all for change. We were for changing the way programmers thought about programming, a narrow topic I must admit, but one with far reaching consequence.

In a decade my wiki site grew to 30,000 pages exploring all aspects of our agenda, thinking people could engage with this material at whatever pace they could muster. Over periods of months, or sometimes years, our critics would evolve. They would say: (1) you're crazy, (2) maybe you're not so crazy, (3) I'm going to try some of these ideas, and then they would say, (4) wow, I've just had some amazing experiences that I have to tell you about.

This is the awesome power of community.

About a year into this journey I called a meeting for wiki authors at OOPSLA, our big programming conference. Attendees could have talked about any of a hundred aspects of my grand experiment. But one thing was on their mind. The question each one asked was, how can they get their peers to collaborate with the agility that they saw on my wiki? How could they make their own wiki work?

Not only had my activist agenda been served by wiki, but wiki itself had surfaced as a worthy agenda in its own right.

There is a special magic that happens when people collaborate. Collaboration touches on our human nature in a way that is easily felt but not so easily explained.

There is also a lot of un-magic going around that prevents us from collaborating. We've made our world out of layer upon layer of things to learn. We've exceeded our own capacity to know and that makes our world a frightening place. From that fear comes self-doubt that disconnects us from what we do know and makes us too cautious to push our world forward.

This book and the companion website dispel the mystery that surrounds Wiki's collaborative abilities. This isn't so much different than the problem I faced when I wanted to change programming. My ideas seemed crazy to those unwilling to give them a try. My wiki site gave them the confidence to push past this and some good tips on moving forward.

This book is organized as a series of case studies. These are the stories of the people who have made wiki work in situations closer to your own than mine. This book backs that up with clear explanations from an author sympathetic to the confusion and sometimes plain fear that is associated with actively changing any group's collaborative culture. Finally the book quotes *Wiki Patterns* from the companion website. These are essentially tips that have been given a name so that they can be discussed, remembered, and employed over and over again.

I dedicated my first wiki to the *Patterns of Programming*. The word "pattern" here has a technical meaning among design theorists. Theorists might argue about what is or isn't a pattern and how what is a pattern should be written. Although I've engaged in those arguments myself, I chose to relax most of the theory behind patterns in favor of attracting more practitioners to the conversation. It worked for me and it works here, too.

My simplification works because it substitutes interested people for the elements of theory. The theory claims to know something about how people acquire, convey, and deploy practical solutions to the problems they are sure to face. A pattern form must be rigorous if the patterns are to stand on their own. We can relax the rigor when we have real people close at hand.

So this is your charter: Assemble interested people and put your first wiki in front of them. Look to the case studies for inspiration in the beginning, but rely on the patterns for insight as you go forward. You will see the most powerful patterns mentioned throughout the book, but you will want to consult the website for more patterns as you and your community gain more experience.

I have faith that you can do it. It's natural, after all, for people to collaborate. The wiki will serve as your community's short-term memory. Study your wiki's pages so that you know what is on your community's mind. Look for creeping complexity and simplify. Look for fear or doubt and summarize. Know that your community will be reading the same pages over and over and with time the pages will become familiar and their subjects less forbidding.

I have faith in your community. As the pages of your wiki drift to and fro, you will find that your community's resolve strengthens, the opposite of what you might expect of answers that wobble a little as they are brought forth. You must trust your community to produce the best that they can, and then better that. This is the magic we call emergence. It is the collective problem solving that early man did in the hunt on the savanna. Today it is harder and must change faster, but we're up to it and have these awesome computers to help.

I will close with a pattern that sums up this foreword. I'll call it the "Wiki" pattern. It is written in "Portland Form," which consists of a problem and solution separated by the connecting word, "therefor."

Our complex culture demands creative decisions from larger proportions of the workforce yet this same complexity robs folks of the confidence to make timely choices. Therefor,

Create an idea-sharing environment where incomplete can be linked together and from this, creative solutions emerge.

Ward Cunningham
Portland, 2007

Acknowledgments

No book is ever really written by one person. I'd like to thank the following people for listening to me talk incessantly about the promise and excitement of wikis, encouraging me to go one step further and write down everything I've been saying for the past several years, and contributing some of the best case studies and examples of wiki use I've seen yet.

I had the great fortune of making a connection with Atlassian in 2006 and it turned out to be one of the most important milestones in both my previous book, *Using Wiki in Education* (wikiineducation.com), and this project. Several people at Atlassian deserve special thanks for their support, involvement, and encouragement of this project.

Jon Silvers, Atlassian's Director of Online Marketing, is one of those rare people who gives generously of his time, expertise, and effort, and expects little fanfare in return. Back in 2006, when I told Jon I was putting together a book on the uses of wiki in education, he put me in touch with several people who ended up contributing chapters, arranged for Atlassian to contribute a copy of Confluence so I could have development of the book take place on a wiki, and arranged for Mike Cannon-Brookes, Atlassian's co-Founder, to write a foreword that helped give people a big picture sense of where the wiki idea came from and how it impacts education.

Not long after that book was finished, Jon gave me the opportunity I'd dreamt of — a chance to help a much broader audience realize the potential of wikis, get the most out of them, and change their organizations for the better. Shortly after I became Atlassian's Wiki Evangelist in January 2007, we launched Wikipatterns.com to provide a hub for all wiki users, and soon after that I began writing this book. Jon is a selfless, willing, and valuable collaborator and I can truly say that without his involvement this book would not be what it is today. Thanks, Jon.

Special thanks to a few others at Atlassian: Jeffrey Walker, for offering sage advice and a sounding board for my ideas; Eugene Katz, for his keen insight and valuable suggestions along the way; and Brittany Walker, for helping type my handwritten pages when I took breaks from typing myself, and for being able to decipher my handwriting, which is an especially difficult task!

The case studies interspersed between chapters are vitally important to the purpose of this book because they illustrate the ideas in each chapter and show you how people have applied them to their wiki use. Special thanks to everyone who took the time to share their wiki uses for all of our benefit:

Ward Cunningham, for an inspiring foreword that is a call to action, and a reminder why collaboration is part of human nature. Ward had the vision to create the first wiki, and in doing so, he has given people a tool that responds to our natural tendency to collaborate in a very human way.

David Goldstein and Sarah S. Cox, LeapFrog, for contributing a case study on LeapFrog's wiki use and examples from their wiki tour designed to help new users see how others are using the wiki and get ideas and inspiration for their own use.

Geoffrey Corb, PMP, Johns Hopkins University, for an excellent case study on how JHU has used a wiki to improve communication on large IT projects, store and organize a fast growing body of knowledge, and reduce the flow of documents over email.

Ben Still, Red Ant, for contributing a case study on wiki use in a web design and development firm in Sydney, Australia. Ben shows you how Red Ant uses their wiki to manage the design process, make sure clients are actively involved, and keep projects on track and running smoothly.

Linda Skrocki, Sun Microsystems, for contributing a case study on Sun's wiki use and wiki guidelines. Sun is clearly a thought leader when it comes to social media use in the enterprise. Jonathan's Blog (written by Sun CEO Jonathan Schwartz) is a great example of forward thinking leadership and transparency. I can't wait to see what they do with wikis!

Stephan Janssen, JavaPolis, for telling us about his use of a wiki to organize and serve as the public website for the JavaPolis conference. Enterprising people like Stephan demonstrate that the wiki's uses are limited only by your imagination!

Kevin Flaherty and Ben Elowitz, Wetpaint, for an excellent case study on how fans of a professional soccer club in the UK have created a wiki all about their team, and built a thriving online community in the process.

Jude Higdon, University of Minnesota, for contributing "A Conversation with a WikiChampion." Jude was a contributor to my first book, *Using Wiki in Education*, and I knew he'd be an excellent contributor to this one, too.

Mark Dilley, AboutUs.org, for contributing an excellent example of how unions can use wikis to collaboratively work on contracts. This is yet another example of the reach and impact of the wiki when people find creative ways to use it.

Jeff Calado, for an excellent case study on growing wiki use and unifying collaboration within a division of a large company.

Peter Higgs, Queensland University of Technology, for sharing a fascinating account of how he made a wiki the hub for organizing and managing the information collected for a creative and cultural industry mapping project.

Tom Hillhouse, National Constitution Center, for contributing a case study on using a wiki to power a public, educational website for an American holiday.

Oliver Widder, Geek and Poke (`http://geekandpoke.typepad.com`), for giving me permission to reprint some of his cartoons at the beginning of several chapters. I hope you enjoy them as much as I do!

Amy Sommer, for putting up with the life of a writer these last several months, and lending an outside perspective to the project that helped me make sure the content of this book is approachable and useful.

All of these people have contributed immensely and immeasurably to this book, and for that I offer them a most heartfelt thanks.

San Francisco
September 2007

Introduction

...If leaders drive change, then collaboration powers change. It is only when people collaborate — really effectively collaborate — that they come to the best outcomes, and the best answers. And in the end, while I think it's vitally important how people build their capabilities...what will distinguish your life and your leadership, as you go forward, is less your capability and more your collaboration skills and your character, and what you choose to do.

Carly Fiorina

This book is about change. It is as much a how-to guide for using a wiki as it is a how-to guide for making change happen. Status quo often becomes the norm when the tools available to people are difficult to use, highly structured and only meet a narrow set of needs, and don't elicit a positive emotional connection from the people that use them. The wiki is a product of the idea that change can replace status quo as the norm if people have tools that do respond to their needs, emphasize the importance of people in building and managing knowledge, and maximize the feeling that they're in charge of their own success.

In this book, you'll explore the value of collaborative approaches that emphasize equal responsibility over hierarchy, look at the key differences between Wikipedia and the wikis used by organizations, and explore what makes a wiki different from other tools used for communication and collaboration. Based on my work running large-scale wiki projects and advising organizations on their wiki adoption, I've laid out a plan that shows you how to make the case for a wiki in your organization, run a wiki pilot that builds real, highly relevant examples you can use later on to grow wiki use, drive adoption throughout your organization, and minimize obstacles along the way.

In several chapters, I reference patterns and anti-patterns from `Wikipatterns.com`, the companion wiki and inspiration for this book. In each case, the pattern reference includes a direct link to the website for more information, and a list of people who have contributed to the pattern page on the wiki. Each of these people has played an important role in building the information about each pattern, and this is my way of acknowledging both their individual contributions and the larger role `Wikipatterns.com` plays in this book.

Interspersed with the chapters are case studies. These are intended to give you a look at a variety of wiki uses, from collaboration and knowledge management in large and small businesses and higher education, to a non-profit using a wiki as the platform for a public website, a group building a wiki dedicated to its favorite sports team, and conference organizers using a wiki to manage and host the website for their event.

All of this was written entirely on a wiki, so it's an example of the change it espouses. My first book, *Using Wiki in Education* (`wikiineducation.com`) was also written and published entirely on a wiki, and I believe it's important to "walk the walk" to inform your own use of a tool so that you understand its value from firsthand experience. Wikipatterns is being published in print to provide a guided approach to wiki adoption based around some of the patterns I see most often, and an introduction to the growing directory of patterns on `Wikipatterns.com`. The book is a fixed set of information designed to help people get started, and the wiki picks up where the book leaves off, providing a growing source of ideas and strategies that come directly from the experiences of its community. The versatility of the wiki is present in the fact that it can be used to power a public site like `Wikipatterns.com`, and provide the private space an author needs to put together a book that will ultimately be published in print. Figure 0-1 shows the homepage of the wiki used to put this book together.

Because the book contents were housed together on the wiki instead of in separate text files, I was able to treat the book as a single, coherent product instead of just a set of chapters, which meant that I could develop certain chapters together where it made sense. For instance, Chapters 4 and 5 explain how to run a wiki pilot and drive large-scale adoption, and have a close relationship to each other because the probability of successful large-scale adoption can be helped by a running a wiki pilot, and a wiki pilot is more likely to be successful when you plan and run it with the idea that it will help excite and inform future users about the wiki. So it made sense to develop them together and make sure they communicated this relationship. Working on the wiki also allowed me to go back and make adjustments to different chapters as I thought of new information, details, or relevant examples to add.

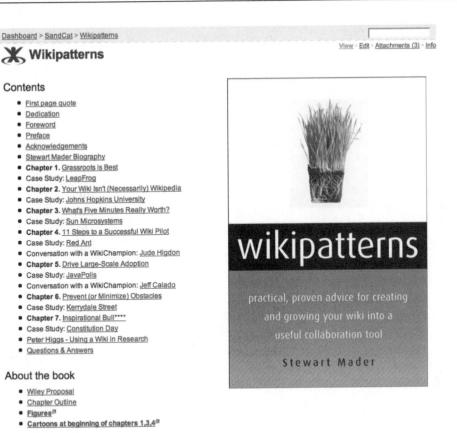

Figure 0-1 Homepage of the wiki used to write this book

The wiki also allowed my editors at Wiley to access the book anytime, subscribe to receive updates via email or RSS so that they could keep up with the latest progress, and leave me in-context feedback in any chapter as they reviewed it.

So the book is not only a strong advocate for wiki use, but is directly connected to and inspired by a wiki (Wikipatterns.com), and is a product of wiki use itself. It demonstrates how the wiki can be embedded into our work in such a way that change becomes a smooth transition, and our work is better for the effort.

San Francisco
September 2007

Wikipatterns

Grassroots is Best

THE CONSULTANTS HANDBOOK PART 7:
SHOW YOUR CUSTOMER THAT YOU ARE THE SMART GUY

geek and poke

Geek and Poke (http:/geekandpoke.typepad.com). Courtesy of Oliver Widder. Used with permission.

In 1950 Eiji Toyoda — cousin of Toyota Motor Corporation founder Kiichiro Toyoda — visited the Ford Rouge plant in Michigan. At the time Toyota had produced 2,685 cars in its entire 13-year history, while Ford produced 7,000 *a day* (Ensici, 2006). He came to see how Ford mass produced cars, in hopes of taking some new ideas back to apply to Toyota's operations.

In the Ford plant, Toyoda saw that the sheet metal parts needed for car assembly were produced using an expensive die stamping system that produced massive quantities of parts, which were stored in warehouses until needed on the assembly line. When the system produced parts with defects, they were set aside to be repaired later, adding more time and expense to the manufacturing process (Ensici, 2006). Toyota didn't have enough money to maintain a system this complex and Toyoda felt it could be made more efficient, so he enlisted the help of Taiichi Ohno, an engineer and machine shop supervisor whose work is now recognized as critical to developing the processes that anchor the famous Toyota Production System (Toyota Motor Manufacturing Kentucky, 2006).

It was on this assignment that Ohno made some critically important discoveries about the role of community and collaboration in improving manufacturing. He concluded that it was better to produce small batches of parts — just enough to cover assembly line needs for the day — because it eliminated storage costs and allowed workers to find and correct defects faster.

> *But to make this system work at all (a system that ideally produced two hours or less of inventory), Ohno needed both an extremely skilled and highly motivated work force. If workers failed to anticipate problems before they occurred and didn't take the initiative to devise solutions, the work of the whole factory could easily come to a halt. Holding back knowledge and effort — repeatedly noted by industrial sociologists as a salient feature of mass production systems — would swiftly lead to disaster in the Toyota plant (Ensici, 2006).*

Ohno's solution was to create small groups of workers, and have them work collaboratively to find the best way to work on their assigned part of the assembly. Instead of the hierarchical system used in mass production where only the foreman had control, each worker was given the power and responsibility to stop the production line if an error was found.

> *By rapidly eliminating the source of the problem, errors did not propagate and multiply through the system as cars moved down the assembly line. In comparison with mass production, as a team of workers becomes more and more accustomed to lean production, the amount of rework required is slashed dramatically (Ensici, 2006).*

So why is this story relevant almost sixty years later? What Toyoda and Ohno did all those years ago transformed Toyota from a small, local automaker into an industry legend that has dominated the global auto industry for decades. By creating a system where every worker had the power to stop the assembly line if they found a problem, the system instilled greater individual responsibility, and gave workers a more direct stake in the success of their work. But even more importantly, the system relied on collaboration among small groups of people to find the best way to do the job, and this is profoundly important.

Instead of giving people a job, and trying to control how they work, it's better to let go: give them the job, and let them figure out the best way to do it.

That's the principle that guided Ohno and Toyoda, and it's the same principle that guides wiki use.

The outcome is what matters, not the method. Not only is the end result better, but it's not just a flash in the pan. It's something sustainable. And isn't that what every organization wants?

When groups work together to find the best way to get a job done, the high quality of work is sustainable because they're finding out the best about themselves, combining individual complimentary strengths and talents, and refining their methods at a very high level. Because they control how they work, people are more self-reflective, constructively critical of their own work, and motivated to make the best contribution possible because they take greater pride in the quality of their work.

So what's the problem?

Collaboration is more important than ever to the success of organizations, growth of economies, and solving some of society's most complex problems, but the knowledge tools in use today fall short of these goals because they don't let groups efficiently work together, are too structured, and are built around a hierarchical, command-and-control structure.

Take email, for example. It's the most ubiquitous tool in organizations, and is often used to send a document around to a group for collaborative editing. Because the document is sent as an attachment, each person makes changes to a separate copy of the document, which means that at some point some really tedious work is required to assemble all the separate edits into one copy of the document. Never mind the mechanical issues; just think of the political issues that can arise if people have differing viewpoints.

Also, errors made by one person might propagate in a document that's emailed around to each collaborator, and might not get fixed until the person who has to combine edits either finds the errors or is made aware of them. Worse yet, the errors might get fixed in some copies, but not others.

This is a nightmare that happens every day in organizations, and the deeper effect is it drives people apart. There's more incentive to dig in your heels and fight for your viewpoint to be preserved in a document you edited in isolation, and so groups have a much harder time achieving cohesion and a strong mutual desire to produce the highest quality work.

Wiki?

Unlike email, which "pushes" discrete copies of the same information to each person, and then requires that the separate revisions be somehow combined, wiki "pulls" people together to work on the same text. Instead of separate copies for each person, everyone looks at the same text on a page, and can immediately make changes directly on that page. Everyone else can see those changes as soon as they're made, which allows each person to better take others' contributions into account as they edit. It also means that information gets created faster because the technical barriers — such as downloading an attachment, opening it (and having the right software to do so!), and then reattaching it to email and sending it on to other collaborators — are minimized.

Errors can be fixed immediately by anyone who notices them, and differing viewpoints can be worked out in a more natural manner. People can work together to reach a balance of viewpoints through a dialog that takes place as they edit, instead of putting forth versions that each feels is final.

The wiki is rapidly growing in name recognition and use in organizations because its simple design and function enables equal participation by people at all levels of technology knowledge and savvy. On top of that, it has an unprecedented ability to adapt to different uses, bring people together and strengthen teams, and promote a collaborative approach to problems.

A wiki is simply a website in which users can create and collaboratively edit pages, and easily link them together. The basic idea behind a wiki is that anyone who can view a page can just as easily edit it and save his or her changes. Enterprise wikis build on the basic wiki idea by including certain functionality that meets the needs of organizations, such as the ability to easily create and manage many individual wiki sites for teams, projects, and departments. Enterprise wikis also include strict security to protect confidential information, fine-grained permissions so that people can be given access to appropriate spaces and pages, and can be tied to other enterprise services via LDAP authentication and single sign-on. These features enable the wiki to mimic the existing social and organizational patterns in departments, teams and projects.

The first wiki, WikiWikiweb (http://c2.com/cgi/wiki?WelcomeVisitors), was created in 1995 by Ward Cunningham to document and collaboratively update information on software design patterns. Since then, wiki has grown steadily into one of the most important tools in today's enterprise, and has become a fixture in popular culture thanks to the rapid rise and increasing influence of Wikipedia. It's commonly thought of today as a so-called Web 2.0 tool because of its proximity to blogs and social networks, but this is primarily because its popularity and name recognition has taken off in tandem with the Web 2.0 phenomenon.

Wiki is the Hawaiian word for quick. According to Cunningham, he chose the words Wiki Wiki, or Wiki (short version), to describe this new tool after remembering that a counter agent at Honolulu International Airport had directed him to take the Wiki Wiki bus to travel between airport terminals, and had explained that wiki is the word meaning "quick" in Hawaiian (Cunningham, 2005). According to Cunningham in 2005, "I wanted an unusual word to name what was an unusual technology. I was not trying to duplicate any existing medium, like mail, so I didn't want a name like electronic mail (email) for my work."

What makes a wiki unique is that it enables multiple people to see and collaboratively edit the same document, in the same "place." Here's where the wiki really resembles that Hawaiian bus service it was named for. People can easily come and go — some might make a small edit which is akin to riding the bus route for just one or two stops, while others might create new pages or make significant contributions and revisions to an existing one, much like traveling the entire route on the bus. The wiki, like the bus itself, enables people to inhabit the same space, namely the page, and see the same thing, namely the text they are all editing, at the same time.

The previous example demonstrates the power of the wiki to make collaboration more inclusive and knowledge construction efficient, distributed, and fast. If you think about this visually, the email/attached document scenario has limited periods of creativity separated by the logistical and socially sensitive task of combining edits. The wiki completely changes this by shifting logistics to the shortest possible segment of time at the outset, leaving a much greater period of time for collaborative creativity and knowledge construction.

The Wikipedia Factor

The Web is becoming a place for the collaborative construction of information on an incredible scale, and the wiki is at the center of this transformation. Almost anyone you meet has heard of Wikipedia, and people are increasingly seeing how the wiki combines simplicity and power in a radically different, paradigm shifting way. In fact, I might venture to say that the wiki is the most significant development on the Internet since the web browser. Where the web browser enabled people to access online information in a radically different and better way that sparked the widespread growth of the Internet, the wiki enables people to directly and easily edit information in a way that encourages increasing participation and exponentially faster growth of online information. In essence, we are moving from passive readers to active participants.

For many people, the first exposure to a wiki is Wikipedia and at times this creates misconceptions about what a wiki is and how it can be used. One common misconception is that it can only be used as an encyclopedia. There's a major fear about privacy of information, or the perceived lack thereof in wikis, because Wikipedia is a completely open wiki where anyone can see any page, even without logging in. Security and integrity of information is another big concern. Because Wikipedia resides on the open Web, people assume that if they used a wiki for internal collaboration anyone could change the information on any page, even if their edits result in inaccurate or completely erroneous information. The reality is quite different when a wiki is used inside an organization, and we'll explore these issues in the next chapter.

You Can Do It!

To successfully grow your wiki into a collaboration and knowledge hub in your organization, the best way to start is with a grassroots, or bottom-up, strategy. The success of a wiki depends on building active, sustainable participation and this happens only when people see that the software is simple enough to be immediately useful, and meets their needs without requiring them to spend lots of extra time learning and using it.

Suw Charman advocates for the same approach and in ''An adoption strategy for social software in the enterprise,'' she makes the point that grassroots adoption is better than mandated adoption in the long run because mandated adoption can slow down, ''if the team leader stops actively making subordinates use the software.'' This is absolutely true, and is one of the major reasons other enterprise content management and knowledge management tools have failed. We'll look at this in more depth in Chapter 3.

To start grassroots adoption, the best approach is to start with a pilot in which a set of groups is given early access to the wiki to start building their collaborative spaces. Along the way, their use can be advised and nurtured by a WikiChampion to help them make it as successful as possible, and this process can be documented to show future users the benefits of wiki use.

If you're the WikiChampion, congratulations! You're the most important person to the wiki, and have the most impact on its future within your organization, especially at the early stages when it's essential to convince people to try it. Encouraging others to do so will give the wiki its first chance to prove itself, and they'll have the greatest probability of success if you encourage the right patterns of behavior and content creation.

Unleash the Early Adopters

Put a wiki into your environment, and you'll probably only have to ask others to use it once (maybe twice). After getting the hang of it and finding that it becomes essential to their work, users become the new wiki coordinators themselves. Often they'll do your asking for you by asking their peers to participate, too. Volunteers are your champions; you just need to give them a nudge!

A wiki has the best probability of success when it gains grassroots support, and people respond well when they see peers actively using and evangelizing it. Don't mandate wiki use; make it available, and then let people find where it's most useful to their work. If they find a new way of doing something, embrace it with an open mind. It may just be an incredibly valuable improvement.

Let people find their natural roles. Some may be interested in gardening the wiki, that is, maintaining and organizing the site; others may want to help grow its use. By letting people lead wiki growth and feel a genuine sense of ownership over their work, you lay the foundation for it to become a successful collaboration tool.

Move Swiftly and with Purpose, but Don't Rush It

One of the biggest mistakes an organization can make is to ignore the new generation of collaboration and its value, but an equally dangerous mistake is to rush into things and forget to give people time to adjust to the new ways of working with tools like wikis. It takes time to gather content that's spread around in disparate places and gradually move it to a wiki, and simultaneously shift existing practices like collaboration over email to wiki-based collaboration.

Be patient when you introduce a wiki to your organization. Some of the payoff won't be immediately apparent because it takes time for people to change the way they work, so it's more important at the beginning to focus on getting broad support and organic growth from all across the organization. Once people see that wiki collaboration actually replaces less effective uses of other forms of communication, such as trying to collaboratively edit a document via email, and gets things done faster, growth will follow.

Using a wiki doesn't mean you have to abandon the tools you're already using. Trying to replace everything else too quickly with the wiki might lead to its downfall if it's not the right solution. It takes time for people to get used to the wiki and find the best uses for it, so when you make it available let it work alongside everything else. Find ways to blend it with what you currently do (for example, some tools let you subscribe to an RSS feed or email update on changes to the wiki), and it won't feel like yet another thing clamoring for your attention.

It Doesn't Matter Where You Are

At Atlassian, the company that develops the Confluence wiki (and where I work as Wiki Evangelist), we have offices in Sydney, San Francisco, and Kuala Lumpur, and one wiki for everyone. This makes it easier to put information in one place where everyone has access and the ability to offer input. For a global company, we're all in close touch and able to communicate, make decisions, and work across these great distances very quickly.

The general idea here is that no matter where in the world you're based, the wiki doesn't just have to be used by people in close proximity to each other — it can bring those who are far away much closer together, to everyone's benefit.

Listen

Most enterprise collaboration and knowledge management software is geared to perform only the functions necessary to the bottom line. This makes it attractive to the "bean-counters" who hold the purse strings, but not to the people who will actually use it. Here, again, the wiki is different because of the absence of rigid structure — besides just having wiki pages for projects, meetings, and so on, people can also have pages for personal profiles, blogs, and even to organize a lunch outing! These pages are a gold mine for people's ideas, opinions, and progress on their work. You'll probably be better informed about your people and projects than ever before, and you can offer feedback, which shows them you're listening and taking them seriously.

Furthermore, profile pages can be useful as a standard place to find contact information, people's biographies (for leadership and public facing employees, this is a great way to always have the most up-to-date bios for trade publications, conferences, and so on), and can be a great place for them to keep links to the project pages they're working on.

Be Open Minded

Renegade thinking is critical to success, but most often the tools an organization selects can spur or damper thinking. The wiki allows for informal, unstructured collaboration, where right-brain thinking thrives. It does away with the rigid structure in a lot of other collaboration and knowledge management tools, and lets people use it as they see fit. There's room for greater innovation, and if the wiki is brought in by renegades, then it's very likely that its success will have much to do with their enthusiasm for it.

In the same way that a wiki is the means to collaboration, it could also be viewed as the product of collaboration. What about using a wiki as your website? The point being, what a wiki is and how it's used are as much about breaking the rules as it is defining new rules. In fact, this is where the wiki has the potential to have the greatest impact on your organization. When people are given the flexibility to approach how they work as much as they simply approach their work itself, they're likely to find new and better ways to work and these should be rewarded, encouraged, and allowed to spread throughout your organization.

Become Better at What You Do

Alan Kay, the visionary genius behind the graphical user interface, smalltalk programming language, and ARPANET — the predecessor of the Internet — was recently interviewed by *CIO Insight* magazine. In the interview, he discusses what isn't right about personal computing and how we should change our thinking for the next generation of computing. From the interview, entitled "Alan Kay: The PC Must be Revamped — Now":

> *"Engelbart, right from his very first proposal to ARPA (Advanced Research Projects Agency), said that when adults accomplish something that's important, they almost always do it through some sort of group activity. If computing was going to amount to anything, it should be an amplifier of the collective intelligence of groups. But Engelbart pointed out that most organizations don't really know what they know, and are poor at transmitting new ideas and new plans in a way that's understandable. Organizations are mostly organized around their current goals. Some organizations have a part that tries to improve the process for attaining current goals. But very few organizations improve the process of figuring out what the goals should be"* (Alter, 2007).

As I read this, I realized that it's a brilliant argument for why the wiki can be a vital tool for organizations. Because it doesn't define the terms of interaction and collaboration from the outset, and allows structure to be created, modified and removed as needed, the wiki quickly becomes a desirable tool because it "learns" how people work *as* they work, not after the fact. This means it captures more of the actual process, giving them an opportunity to regularly look at how they collaborate, even during a current project.

Think how much more productive a group can be if it sees where it's weak during a project and can correct that weakness on the spot. Now imagine how much more productive an entire organization can become if every group is doing this. Toyoda and Ohno realized this, and didn't just look at how things fit into the assembly line, but thought in terms of the whole strategy. That enabled them to create a whole new way of working that engaged employees, involved their thinking skills instead of just their manual labor skills, and resulted in stronger employee loyalty, lower storage and repair costs, and some of the best products in their industry. You can do the same for the knowledge in your organization using wiki collaboration — that's the promise of collective intelligence realized!

Wiki Patterns and `Wikipatterns.com`

Human behavior is pattern-based, and wikis are designed to support the patterns of activity that occur when groups work together. Therefore, there's no right or wrong way to use a wiki, so it's impossible to write a recipe for successful wiki use that will work in all cases. Instead, documenting the behaviors seen on different wikis and classifying those that help the wiki effort as patterns, and those that hinder the wiki as anti-patterns is a more useful way to offer guidance to other wiki users.

That's why we created `Wikipatterns.com`. Launched in February 2007, `Wikipatterns.com` (Figure 1-1) is intended to give anyone, anywhere, using any wiki software, a collection of these patterns that they can use to ensure the greatest probability of success when introducing a wiki to their organization.

It's organized around two major strands of content. The people patterns and anti-patterns (Figure 1-2) describe the various ways people interact with the wiki, and the patterns detail roles that can be introduced to help a growing wiki. The people anti-patterns describe some behaviors that are not necessarily the result of any ill will or malicious motivation (except for vandalism, perhaps), but are mostly the result of people not understanding how the wiki works and how to be a productive member of the community. To help people remedy these anti-patterns, the pages for each detail ways to curb the anti-pattern behavior and keep the wiki on track.

The adoption patterns and anti-patterns (Figure 1-3) focus on overall organization of the wiki, getting groups started using it, keeping content organized as the wiki grows, making the wiki part of the normal induction for new employees, avoiding empty pages, and determining when to use the wiki versus when to use email.

Each pattern page (Figure 1-4) describes the pattern, explains where it's most used, and gives examples that can help readers relate the pattern to their own wikis. The pages for anti-patterns also include sections on what to look for to recognize the anti-patterns, and how to fix it. Both pattern and anti-pattern pages link to related patterns so readers get a sense of how behaviors on the wiki are connected. In the case of patterns, this can help you find other relevant patterns to apply, and for anti-patterns, it helps you know what other things might also happen on your wiki so that you can be best prepare to catch and fix them if they do.

The patterns and anti-patterns on the site are loosely modeled on the concept of software design patterns — those recurring patterns of behavior that can be recognized and channeled for the good of the team. Patterns are the types of activity that one would want to happen on the wiki, and anti-patterns are the scenarios that should be avoided or fixed to keep the growth of wiki use on track. For instance, the IntentionalError pattern suggests making an obvious mistake that someone else will be so compelled to fix, they just jump in and

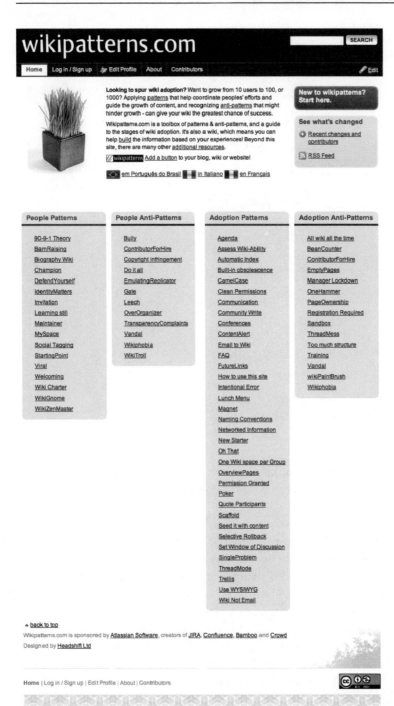

Figure 1-1 Wikipatterns.com

People Patterns	People Anti-Patterns
90-9-1 Theory	Bully
BarnRaising	ContributorForHire
Biography Wiki	Copyright infringement
Champion	Do it all
DefendYourself	EmulatingReplicator
IdentityMatters	Gate
IdentityMatters (IT)	Leech
Invitation	OverOrganizer
Learning still	TransparencyComplaints
Maintainer	Vandal
MySpace	Wikiphobia
Social Tagging	WikiTroll
StartingPoint	
Viral	
Welcoming	
Wiki Charter	
WikiGnome	
WikiZenMaster	

Figure 1-2 People patterns and anti-patterns

do it — and they've edited the wiki! The idea here is that a person's primary motivation when they see an error is to fix it, and the wiki provides an easy, immediate means to do so.

Wikipatterns.com itself is a wiki, and since its launch in February 2007, the site has grown from 29 to 78 patterns. Most of those have been contributed by the 711 registered users that make up the community as of October 2007.

Throughout this book, you'll look at several patterns and anti-patterns, and you'll learn how to apply them to help your own wiki grow. But this book is just a starting point, and Wikipatterns.com is the ongoing community that you can help build. So I invite you to use the site regularly to find useful patterns that can help you in specific situations, and give them a try. Once you've done so, please come back to the site to share your experiences, contribute new patterns, and add anecdotes and examples to the existing patterns. Others in the community will benefit from, and appreciate, the knowledge you contribute, and the community will become richer and more valuable as a result!

Adoption Patterns	Adoption Anti-Patterns
Agenda	All wiki all the time
Assess Wiki-Ability	BeanCounter
Automatic Index	ContributorForHire
Built-in obsolescence	EmptyPages
CamelCase	Manager Lockdown
Clean Permissions	OneHammer
Communication	PageOwnership
Community Write	Registration Required
Conferences	Sandbox
ContentAlert	ThreadMess
Email to Wiki	Too much structure
FAQ	Training
FutureLinks	Vandal
How to use this site	wikiPaintBrush
Intentional Error	Wikiphobia
Lunch Menu	
Magnet	
Naming Conventions	
Networked Information	
New Starter	
Oh That	
One Wiki space per Group	
OverviewPages	
Permission Granted	
Poker	
Quote Participants	
Scaffold	
Seed it with content	
Selective Rollback	
Set Window of Discussion	
SingleProblem	
ThreadMode	
Trellis	
Use WYSIWYG	
Wiki Not Email	

Figure 1-3 Adoption patterns and anti-patterns

Champion

- em Português do Brasil
- in Italiano

What is it?

A passionate, enthusiastic champion is essential to the success of wiki because s/he will be able to generate interest, give the appropriate amount of training for each person at the right time, monitor growth of the tool and fix problems that could derail adoption.

Usage

The champion makes her/himself synonymous with wiki in an organization. When people think of wiki, they immediately think of the champion as the go-to person for guidance on learning the wiki and expanding its use to larger projects, planning events, managing meetings, and capturing tacit knowledge.

Example

A wiki champion is someone who possesses the following traits:

- Thought leader who is a recognized early adopter and respected by peers
- Understands the nature of work involved in project, group, business, etc.
- Understands how to use a wiki - how to organize content, get others involved, make it easy to use and keep it organized as it grows.
- "Gradually they train everyone that information flow, at least as far as they're concerned, happens on the wiki." (from It's on the Wiki!⬚)
- Encourages others, but doesn't push too hard or fast because an All wiki all the time approach can be dangerous, especially at the beginning when people are still learning how to use it.
- Gets people involved by informally training them and being available for ongoing support.

Rate this pattern? ★ ★ ★ ★ ★

Related Patterns

- All wiki all the time - an anti-pattern in which someone pushed for the wiki to be used for everything, all the time. An effective wiki champion will avoid this by pushing the wiki the appropriate amount at the appropriate time, and properly pacing adoption.
- WikiGnome - also known as WikiGardener, a person who keeps the wiki running smoothly by fixing broken links, typos, and improving the overall flow and quality of content. Champions and WikiGnomes are critical to the success and quality of the wiki.
- WikiTroll - someone who tries to disrupt the wiki by posting inflammatory comments and distracting people from the talk at hand. A champion will swiftly deal with the disruptions of a WikiTroll to keep the wiki running smoothly, and try to help the WikiTroll become a more productive community member.
- Maintainer - the Wiki Champion often is the same guy as its maintainer.

Further Reading

- The Wiki Champion @ StructuredWikis⬚
- Wikis at work @ Dice.com⬚
- It's on the Wiki! @ Understanding Nothing⬚

Please Log in or sign-up to discuss the pattern.

People Patterns	People Anti-Patterns	Adoption Patterns	Adoption Anti-Patterns
90-9-1 Theory	Bully	Agenda	All wiki all the time
BarnRaising	ContributorForHire	Assess Wiki-Ability	BeanCounter
Biography Wiki	Copyright infringement	Automatic Index	ContributorForHire

Figure 1-4 A typical pattern page

References

Alter, Alan. "Alan Kay: The PC Must Be Revamped — Now," *CIO Insight*, www.cioinsight.com/article2/0,1540,2089567,00.asp, 14 February 2007 (Retrieved 24 May 2007).

Charman, Suw. "An adoption strategy for social software in enterprise," *Strange Attractor*, http://strange.corante.com/archives/2006/03/05/an_adoption_strategy_for_social_software_in_enterprise.php, 5 March 2006 (Retrieved 24 May 2007).

Cunningham, Ward. Correspondence on the Etymology of Wiki, http://c2.com/doc/etymology.html February, 2005 (Retrieved 25 July 2007).

Ensici, Ayhan. "Frog History Lessons," *Designophy*, www.designophy.com/article.php?id = 29, 19 October 2006 (Retrieved 8 May 2007).

Toyota Motor Manufacturing Kentucky, Inc. "History," *Toyota Motor Manufacturing Kentucky, Inc.*, www.toyotageorgetown.com/history.asp, 2006. (Retrieved 24 May 2007).

Case Study: LeapFrog

LeapFrog Enterprises, Inc.
Emeryville, California, USA
www.leapfrog.com
A Conversation with David Goldstein, Senior Software Engineer — LeapFrog R&D Advanced Concepts
Type of organization: Technology and learning products company
Number of wiki users: 500 currently (first six months of soft rollout), scaling to 1000 (global corporate launch — next six months)
LeapFrog is a leading designer, developer and marketer of innovative, technology-based educational products and related proprietary content. LeapFrog is 100 percent focused on developing products that will provide the most engaging, effective learning experience for all ages, in school or home, around the world. We put learning first — a philosophy that distinguishes us from our competitors and fuels the entire company.

1. Why Did You Choose a Wiki?

In LeapFrog R&D's Advanced Concepts group — a small, multidisciplinary team of researchers, product designers, and engineers — we started looking for an information management system in which to log new product ideas, track concepts over the course of their development, and spark better collaboration between team members.

We initially thought we'd just implement a rudimentary database and get whatever we could up and running in a couple months. But luckily, we had a small window of opportunity to take a step back from our department's immediate need and look at the common information management needs across all company departments to see if we might better leverage our chosen solution. And as is common in many organizations, the more we dug into current corporate practices and requirements, the more we realized how truly entangled and dysfunctional our information system architecture was and what a tremendous drag on corporate efficiency and employee sanity that entailed.

At LeapFrog, company knowledge was being stored in a multitude of information "haystacks" on at least a dozen shared network drives with their G:, H:, L:, and U: mappings, employee's local computer hard drives, at least two informal wikis already set up — one a grassroots product of the software engineering team and the other a commercial hosted solution — employees' email folders, hard drive mirrors and "frozen" email folders of departed employees, a handful of proprietary content management tools, networked Subversion source code repositories, the corporate intranet, and finally (and critically) in each employee's gray matter.

In a matter of weeks, our search for a rudimentary information management system had evolved into much more for us — really a matured philosophy on organizational process and efficiency.

The key project goals that led us to select a wiki as our information management platform at LeapFrog were the desires to:

- Create one central website through which most corporate digital information is accessed.
- Make all that information easily searchable.
- Remove all bottlenecks to information contribution and flow within the company — decentralize information input into the system and enable everyone to be a contributor.
- Have only one, authoritative location for all pieces of information, but allow for many different views of the same information.

The net result promised to provide employees and management with greatly improved access, version control, transparency, and visibility into corporate knowledge, projects, and status.

Thus "Emma" was born — a wiki-based Enterprise Management and Media Archiving platform for LeapFrog.

2.   What Type of wiki are You Using?

Emma is based on a commercial, enterprise wiki built on Java components running on a TomCat installation. The wiki application provides a rich framework for user- or community-developed plug-ins to extend its baseline functionality, which we've taken advantage of to customize the look, feel, and data architecture of our site.

Our wiki is currently deployed inside the corporate firewall for exclusive use by company employees and internal contractors. However, we are getting increasingly frequent requests from business and functional units to provide wiki access outside the firewall to external second- and third-party developers, vendors, and education advisory board members. Our need to support those constituents is inevitable, so we'll be working with our IT department over the next year to securely extend wiki access outside the company.

3.   How Are You Using the wiki?

We purposely branded the internal LeapFrog site with a human name — Emma — instead of using the term *wiki* to give our new web-based application for the company a non-intimidating, friendly face. It was a nice way to focus on what our real *goals* were in introducing a wiki into LeapFrog work life instead of the specific *technology solution*.

Emma is very much a grassroots project at LeapFrog. It was started by and evangelized by a team of two in the LeapFrog R&D Advanced Concepts group — our WikiChampions, but is now fueled by a host of ad hoc resources within the company including an enthusiastic Developer Support & Training team who have taken on "Emma Support," an Emma Users Group, and finally the buy-in of LeapFrog senior staff.

Launching, recruiting, and continuing to nurture a cross-department Emma Users Group has been absolutely key to our wiki's success. Proposing a fundamental overhaul of enterprise information management and, frankly, LeapFrog work culture across a 1000-some person global corporate structure was daunting. The members of the Emma Users Group — originally one "donated" person from each pilot project we ran in the early days — have been key to our leaping the inevitable corporate adoption hurdles. They've served as early adopters, evangelists, decentralized help resources, co-developers, beta testers, and the source for some of our best feature ideas.

Our chosen wiki application allows organizing information into a collection of individual, peer sub-wikis, or "spaces." Each space is like its own wiki website within a larger application framework that allows for seamless page linking and global search across all spaces.

We analyzed the fundamental groups of information we work with at LeapFrog and identified some natural "bins" in which to organize things in the wiki:

- A personal space for each user of the site in which they can do whatever they wish

- A space for each company project

- A space for each organizational group — be it a formal department like HR or Finance, cross-functional team or recreational or interest group like the LeapFrog Running Club or Toastmasters

- A mechanism for building individual project, personal or group FAQs into a collective, site-wide FAQ system

- One space that serves as our collective knowledge base of technical, market, and competitive information — LeapFrog's internal Wikipedia if you will

- One space that provides the site framework, including top-level site navigation, directories and search, along with serving up the main Emma homepage. Emma's homepage includes up-to-date LeapFrog internal and public news, lists of recent site changes, most popular pages and blog posts, and a running blog of site status, known issues, and tips. Using some of our wiki's free developer-community-created plug-ins, Emma users can also personalize their Emma homepage by labeling any page on the site to be a tabbed ad-in panel on the homepage much like Google's customized "iGoogle" tabs.

Within these bins and UI constructs, our wiki has enabled a wide range of streamlined information-sharing tools and policies including:

- Tearing down the walls between functional groups working on the same project. For instance, rather than project specifications being spread across five different department network drives, each with their own unique folder structures and IT-imposed access rights, all Emma projects have a specifications page to which technical, marketing, and project management documents are uploaded with simple tabbed panels that automatically separate the list of specs by functional area.

- What we call "About Boxes" on the homepage of every project, person, and group space on the site — templated, graphic panels that users fill out with names, employee positions and functional responsibilities, contact information, representative icons and photos, project milestones and status, and related information displayed in a uniform manner. Our About Boxes provide users with the key identity of each area of the site.

- A portal to all Subversion source code repositories cross-company and providing their administrative UI.

- Project, team and corporate information dashboards — a much more public and accessible view of key metrics.

- Building a true corporate-wide knowledge base with the ease of simple search-box access — on LeapFrog products, the results of product compatibility evaluations, competitors and their offerings, technologies, vendors, industry resources, educational learning best practices, local restaurants with exceptionally good enchiladas, and much more.

- Enabling employee blogs — giving each employee a voice, visibility, and a chance for the best ideas to rise to the top freed from the typical organizational friction.

- Stoking what we variously call "grassroots," "homebrew," or "ad hoc" projects within the company — allowing innovation to flourish in all corners of the company, and employees to search for and recruit colleagues across the organization with the skills to bring their ideas to fruition.

Emma is designed to be the central portal through which most company digital information is accessed. But we realized how important it was in its adoption to make clear to our colleagues that we didn't expect a wiki to be the appropriate information management tool for everything at LeapFrog. We want to avoid the pattern of All Wiki All the Time. So in pitching Emma at LeapFrog, we always emphasize the following:

- We recognize the importance of our continuing to select the best suited information management tools for any particular enterprise application — such as project tasks, tracking and scheduling, a corporate knowledge base, source code management, or legal and manufacturing document workflow.

- We define LeapFrog's Emma site as a "portal" *through* which we expect most enterprise digital information to be accessed but not necessarily the appropriate end-application for everything. Emma is a Grand Central hub for information rather than a Mecca.

As a result, LeapFrog still makes use of many other best-of-breed enterprise apps including Jira and Test Track Pro for issues and bug tracking, Subversion for source code management, MS Project Server for project management, and Oracle and Agile to manage financials and design and product changes across a set of globally dispersed contract manufacturers, design centers, and packaging centers. And we're in the process of giving many of these a front porch on our wiki.

4. Looking at `Wikipatterns.com`, What Patterns are in Use on Your wiki?

What became clear very early in our project was wiki adoption and use is most definitely a social sciences project as much as one of information management. We've found many of the patterns and anti-patterns described in Wikipatterns were part of our early proposals on the role and rollout of LeapFrog's wiki — Emma — or have shown up on their own in the wild as Emma's been more widely deployed.

From the list of People Patterns, the ones that are most relevant to our usage are *BarnRaising, Champion, Invitation, Maintainer, MySpace, StartingPoint, Viral*, and *WikiZenMaster*. Thankfully we've managed to avoid the known People Anti-Patterns.

Among Adoption Patterns, we've made use of a laundry list including *Agenda, Automatic Index, Communication, Community Write, ContentAlert, Email to Wiki, FAQ, FutureLinks, How to Use this Wiki, Lunch Menu, Magnet, Naming Conventions, Networked Info, New Starter, One Wiki Space per Group, Overview-Pages, Permission Granted, Poker, Scaffold, Selective Rollback, Single Problem, ThreadMode, WYSIWYG*, and *Wiki not Email*.

Adoption Anti-Patterns we've actively had to contend with include *All Wiki All the Time, Empty Pages, OneHammer, Training*, and *WikiPaintBrush*.

5. What Changes Have You Seen As a Result of Using a wiki?

We're about three months from full corporate rollout of our wiki, so the largest cultural changes are still down the road for us. But our window into the effect Emma's having at LeapFrog includes:

- There's a growing emphasis on the efficiency of information creation and distribution, and on its quality and utility rather than getting tied up in presentation-ready aesthetics (for example, Microsoft Word and Adobe PDF). A boon for corporate efficiency.

- Cross-functional project teams are beginning to work more as unified teams than task silos on the project schedule.

- The "Emma" branding is working — it's becoming part of our standard lexicon, and a viral term for introducing Emma to new users as managers now announce at meetings that support docs will be put on Emma as a follow-up.

- The wiki has placed information front and center at a time when executive staff was searching for ways to make our decision-making processes more transparent and accessible.

- Our Emma Users Group, with its biweekly meetings, now seems to be single-handedly propping up the local donut shop.

Finally, a senior exec recently challenged us to come up with utilities and other features that would speed adoption of our wiki. Tossing this to our Emma Users Group one week, their response is very telling of the benefits a well-thought-out wiki implementation can have in the corporate environment and what you might harness to capture the imagination and investment of employees:

- LFN (LeapFrog Food Network) — mount wireless web cameras in our kitchens with live feeds to the Emma home page so employees know when free food is available. Bonus points for adding signs saying "place food on this table to be rapidly disposed of" and integrating an image recognition package to notify employees of the specific presence of donuts or similar circular-shaped consumables.

- Employee Finder — is your network stack guru not at her desk? Use the Adobe Flash wiki plug-in to man the controls of the 4-foot long, camera-toting, remote-control blimp and determine her location in the suite. Bonus points for building a wiki forms interface to the on-board LED sign.

- Ping Pong Table Leader Board and Live Action Cam.

- Incorporate employee-generated buy/sell banner ads.

- Have HR develop a comprehensive set of wiki resources for new-employee settlement in the San Francisco Bay Area.

- Auto-generate an interactive, hyper-linked company org chart — since employees fill out their About Boxes in Emma with their manager's name, one homebrew project we've already started with some free wiki-developer-community plug-ins is auto-generating and auto-updating a full organizational chart of LeapFrog. This promises to save our HR department countless hours of quarterly work.

So these are clearly high on our priority list.

Your Wiki Isn't (Necessarily) Wikipedia

"Have you heard of a wiki?"
"No."
"Have you heard of Wikipedia?"
"Oh, yes!"

I'm reminded of Wikipedia's importance both as a wiki and a cultural phenomenon each time I have this exchange with someone. Wikipedia has democratized participation and changed the way people think about building and accessing knowledge like nothing before it, save for the printing press. For me, it helps establish a frame of reference to explain what a wiki is and how it can be used in organizations.

Wikipedia is one example of how wiki collaboration can be used: to build an encyclopedia. In my experience, it's one of the lesser-used applications in organizations. Whereas an encyclopedia makes sense for a large social community, other uses make more sense inside organizations where needs and priorities are different.

But because it is the most well-known example of a wiki, people new to the idea of using a wiki in an organization or enterprise can be highly influenced by Wikipedia's pattern of use, and think that wiki use in their organization will be fraught with all the pitfalls of Wikipedia they've heard about in the news. The reality is, Wikipedia is quite different from organizational wiki sites both because of its primary use — encyclopedia — and the way its community is structured. I often say it's the most extreme instance of wiki in existence because everyone can see its entire contents, anyone can contribute, and people can do so anonymously.

These characteristics have made Wikipedia successful, but they aren't necessarily the conditions for success for every wiki. Most organizations can't have content publicly viewable, nor can they even have it viewable by everyone within the organization. Editing often needs to be restricted to specific people or teams, and anonymity isn't necessary because people on a team already know each other; so knowing who's editing a document enables discussion among the people collaborating on the document and allows people to be given credit for the changes they've made.

Brief History of Wikipedia

Wikipedia was initially set up as a feeder project for Nupedia, an online encyclopedia founded by Jimmy Wales in early 2000. Wales wanted articles in Nupedia to be of similar quality to other professionally edited encyclopedias, so the site tried to get experts to write articles and use a peer review process to vet them for accuracy. Along the way, Wikipedia was set up as a place to start and collaboratively develop articles destined for the peer review process. Because of the lower barrier to entry on Wikipedia, it quickly outpaced Nupedia in number of articles and contributors, and has grown rapidly into the tour de force it is today.

Wikipedia took off because it enabled communities to organically spring up around common interests, and collaboratively author the corresponding articles about them. Nupedia focused first on the information, and as a result it limited itself by only wanting experts to write articles. That reduced the pool of potential contributors on any topic, and complicated the authoring process with questions of how to verify the expertise of contributors. Wikipedia inherently focused on people from the start, by using the wiki to make article creation easier, and that's why it has taken off so quickly.

This raises the question of accuracy. Nupedia tried to ensure accuracy up front by looking for experts to write articles. Wikipedia has achieved accuracy because the process is a self-checking one. The low barrier to entry of the wiki means that not only can articles be created quickly, but also the presence of an interested community results in accurate information and rapid error correction.

Jon Udell's "Heavy metal umlaut: the movie" illustrates this very well; in it, he shows the history of content growth on the Wikipedia entry on the use of the umlaut in heavy metal band names (Udell, 2005). In one example, he shows how the community editing the page experimented with various ways to represent names that use the umlaut, from code tricks to the use of LaTeX document markup, to the eventual use of an image of the SpinalTap logo. The initial methods didn't work well, and the community editing the page reacted quickly to try new ideas.

At another point in the video, he shows how a vandal defaced the page, and within less than a minute another editor restored the page to its previous state. This continued on for several minutes, with the vandal defacing the page, and an editor immediately restoring the page, until the vandal gave up and stopped altering the page. This illustrates the commitment interested communities have to the pages they edit, and the resulting high level of accuracy and integrity they can maintain on a publicly editable page.

Nature Compares Accuracy of Wikipedia and Britannica

A 2005 study by the journal *Nature* has provided some support of this, by concluding that for science topics Wikipedia is about as accurate as Britannica (Giles, 2005). To conduct the study, *Nature* asked its journalists to choose articles from Wikipedia and Encyclopaedia Britannica on the topics they regularly cover. They stripped out any identifying information about which encyclopedia the articles had come from, then sent them to experts in each topic for blind comparison.

For the 42 topics compared, Wikipedia was found to have an average of four errors or inaccuracies per article, while Britannica was found to have an average of three. The journal's conclusion was that the quality of the information in the two, at least for science topics, was about equal. Even though Wikipedia articles had, on average, one more error than Britannica articles, people editing those articles could fix the errors immediately, thanks to the wiki. The people publishing Britannica, however, would have to wait until the next edition of their encyclopedia was revised and published to fix their errors.

Ironically it took Britannica three months to reply, and in the reply they accused *Nature* of conducting faulty research. *Nature* issued a detailed rebuttal to Britannica, with point-by-point responses to Britannica's complaints, but Britannica has already illustrated a bigger point. In its initial report, *Nature* said, "It is going to take Britannica longer than Wikipedia to deal with this issue," and by taking three months to even reply and make a statement about it, Britannica confirmed this.

The study also addressed high-profile media coverage of some incidents where Wikipedia pages were edited with false or misleading information. "One article was revealed as falsely suggesting that a former assistant to U.S. Senator Robert Kennedy may have been involved in his assassination. And podcasting pioneer Adam Curry has been accused of editing the entry on podcasting to remove references to competitors' work. Curry says he merely thought he was making the entry more accurate. However, an expert-led investigation carried out by *Nature* — the first to use peer review to compare Wikipedia and Britannica's coverage of science — suggests that such high-profile examples are the exception rather than the rule" (Giles, 2005).

In an editorial published in the same issue of *Nature* as the study, the editors reflected on the growing importance of Wikipedia and the potential result if it further closed the gap with highly respected rival reference works: "a comprehensive, accurate and up-to-date reference work that can be accessed free from Manhattan to rural Mongolia" (*Nature*, 2005). Whether or not this can happen, they argued, hinges on finding contributors who can further refine the quality of entries, and they called on their own readership to help, arguing that "... scientists can bring a critical eye to entries on subjects they study, often highlighting errors and misunderstandings that others have unintentionally introduced" (*Nature*, 2005).

By conducting this study, *Nature* shed light on an issue that was, until that point, receiving inaccurate coverage because of a general lack of understanding of Wikipedia, and the propensity of the media to highlight a newsworthy story even if it's the exception and not the norm. The ensuing debate was equally eye-opening because there are plenty of people who think that the wiki is a passing fad, or don't know what to think of it, or think that maybe there were flaws in *Nature*'s work. And there may have been; but the impact of it on the people's thinking is what is really important, and no matter what people think of it, it has made a big impact. There has been a lot of talk about the idea since that study, and now more and more research is emerging on the idea of looking at what happens in the revision history of a wiki page, versus material that is published in more static book form.

When you pick up an article in Britannica and read the content, you get what's there at face value but you don't know what went into developing that article. There's no easy way for you to know the backgrounds, influences, and biases of the authors. Now think about reading that article on Wikipedia. You'd have not only the article itself, but the revision history that reveals the social forces behind the construction of that article. You can see, for instance, where authors may have disagreed about the content, when people have contributed new content, and who those people might be. Although you can edit anonymously, some people want their names attached to their work. The bottom line is, with a wiki you see not only the end product of the information, but you get to see the construction of that knowledge, and that's incredibly valuable in measuring the quality of that information.

It's that ability to easily edit, refine, and even repair information that's at the heart of not just Wikipedia, but the wiki concept. But it's important to understand the significant differences between how the wiki is used as the foundation for Wikipedia, and how it's used in organizations.

The All-Virtual Wiki Community versus Wiki that Mirrors Physical Community

When comparing organizations' wikis and Wikipedia, I often say there are two types of wiki communities — the all-virtual versus the wiki that mirrors a physical community. Wikipedia exemplifies the all-virtual community, where contributors belong to the community only through their participation on the site. This can lead to some of the perceived problems with Wikipedia, such as vandalism of entries on popular or hotly contested issues, posting of rude or hostile comments to other users (flaming), or people and organizations editing entries to serve their interests. For example, Microsoft got into hot water with the blogosphere earlier this year because it allegedly offered to pay a blogger to edit Wikipedia entries on the XML protocol that it perceived to have an anti-Microsoft sentiment (Jeliffe, 2007).

The wiki in your organization is the second kind because people are part of the community for more reasons than just the wiki. They either work or volunteer for the organization, they regularly work with a known group of people and they are often working toward a common goal. They may be in close proximity (even the same office) with at least some of the people they work with, but may be at great distances or even have never met others they work with, but the effects of this are quite different than in an all-virtual group, and the wiki will be used in ways that support the overarching goals of the organization.

Why Mischief Doesn't Happen in an Organization's Wiki

Upon first hearing about the wiki as a workplace tool, some people think that it will be as open and anonymous as Wikipedia or worse yet, an uncontrolled mess with no productive use and lots of inappropriate behavior. For people used to communication that seems more controlled, like conversations, meetings, and email, this can be very disconcerting.

The reality is, this just doesn't happen. Let's look at some reasons why.

Open versus Secure

Wikipedia is a very open, public site and even allows anonymous editing because that's what works best for its community. For most people, Wikipedia is the first experience they have with editing a live web page, so having the fewest possible barriers to entry is critical. Giving people the ability to edit something immediately, and even anonymously, is what gets them to fix an error, or add a new piece of information to an article.

The anonymity does increase the potential for people to vandalize the site or use it as a soapbox for their views on a topic, but those negative effects have to be taken in context. When the news media makes a big story out of a "Wikipedia scandal" like the incident where someone edited the comedian Sinbad's entry to say he had a heart attack, the reality is that's just one edit and there were thousands, maybe millions, of edits that same day that were perfectly legitimate and added new or more accurate information to the wiki. The media often "forgets" to mention this, because putting it in context detracts from the supposed newsworthiness of the story.

In the wiki of a private organization, this kind of vandalism or erroneous editing is extremely unlikely to happen because the wiki is being used within an already established social and organizational structure. The fact is people just don't abuse tools that are important to their professional work.

It's important to strike a balance between openness and security. Keeping the wiki open to a point where people can collaborate across teams might be a little less secure than restricting each team to its own space, but it's likely to help people realize the interplay between the work of different teams and work even more closely. This can make your organization dramatically more efficient. At the same time, users need to know that they can use permissions to control access at several levels, depending on their requirements.

Quality, Accuracy, and Moderators

Because the accuracy of Wikipedia is questioned regularly in the media, many new users reflect that when they question the accuracy of the new wiki you're evangelizing in your organization. It might be useful to point out the *Nature* study and its conclusion that Wikipedia is quite accurate. But it's important to address Wikipedia and then put it aside to focus on your wiki.

New users need to understand that the wiki is merely a tool, as is their email, their word processor, or anything they use to do their work. The wiki is no more or less accurate than these other tools. It is simply a new mechanism. The social nature of the wiki actually offers the opportunity to have higher accuracy.

When an organization wants to verify accuracy of information on a wiki page, the page might include a ContentAlert. This is a standard message posted at the top of the page indicating that the page needs to have information added, sources cited, or a section checked for accuracy.

How Will Your Wiki Be Used?

The wiki can be applied to a wide variety of specific uses that are fundamentally different from an encyclopedia. New users benefit from seeing a variety of applications — sales processes, technical documentation, work group collaboration, event planning, and so on — so that they can visualize how they might use the wiki. One of the first steps is to show new users these possibilities.

Build a Peer Directory

Keeping an up-to-date employee directory is a constant challenge for many organizations. When people join, leave, change roles, or move to a new office information needs to be updated accordingly. In reality, this doesn't always happen in a timely manner, so the organization directory gets out of date, and you only find out when you try to call someone and find out they haven't worked for your company in a year!

Creating a wiki-based peer directory can be an ideal solution because it distributes the responsibility to update personal information to the people themselves. It also gives people a reason to come to the wiki in the first place — to put their information in the directory — and then they stay to collaborate. Building a Facebook-style page can be a great first experience editing the wiki, because it helps people tackle the paradigm shift of an editable website in stages. Unlike a meeting agenda or project document, someone else isn't likely to edit your personal information, so this gives people a chance to get used to the process of wiki editing. Later on, when they start collaborating with others, they're likely to be more comfortable with making changes and seeing changes made to their work if they're already proficient, confident editors themselves.

Agendas → Meetings → Projects

If you email a meeting agenda to a group of people, and then find that something needs to be changed, you have to make changes and send another email. Likewise, if someone else needs to change the agenda, they'll have to either email you to ask that the change be made, or do it themselves and resend the agenda to the group. In either case, there's a possibility that with so many versions of the agenda circulating each person will come to the meeting with a different agenda!

Instead of emailing the agenda, put it on a wiki page and email people a link to that page. If changes need to be made, anyone can do so and everyone will have immediate access to the same, up-to-date version. Then, record minutes on the wiki so all information pertaining to the meeting is in one place. The further advantage here is that the responsibility to take minutes doesn't have to rest with just one person. No matter how carefully one person listens and takes notes, it's really difficult for one person to accurately capture everything that happens during the course of a meeting. One person may pick up on a certain detail that another person misses, so using the wiki can give everyone a place to contribute, resulting in a more comprehensive account of the meeting.

Keeping meeting agendas and minutes on the wiki can be the perfect foundation for project and task management. As various topics and items from a meeting are discussed and need further action, new wiki pages can spawn from the agenda or minutes and be used to manage them.

Manage Projects

Give each project a page in your wiki, and keep all relevant materials there. One way this may happen is as a result of the project being discussed and approved in a meeting, so project pages may organically grow out of meeting minutes. This is a great example of how the wiki can flexibly adapt to how your organization works.

It's a huge timesaver to have everything in one place and easily updated, and it ensures that everyone associated with the project has consistent information. Furthermore, if the project management pages have grown out of meeting agendas and minutes, reporting on project progress becomes part of a cycle that's fully captured on the wiki. This allows greater flexibility with the information because it can be referenced in other areas of the wiki, like an annual report or strategic plan, or other projects.

Product Development

A wiki is ideal for managing your organization's products from development to production, marketing, and support. The product designers and engineers might start by collaborating on the design, features, and technical specifications for the product. The manufacturer could then be invited to the wiki to be involved in the discussions on issues like materials and production processes. When the designers and engineers make changes, the wiki allows the manufacturer to know immediately and change manufacturing processes accordingly.

You can also invite other groups such as marketing and support to the wiki to collaborate on developing marketing materials and offer input based on experience with customers. Marketing staff can also use product information from the wiki to develop the marketing campaign, product materials, and website content. Support people can offer input on the product based on common issues they've seen with earlier or similar products, and by being involved on the wiki, they'll have a more thorough knowledge of the product as they support customers.

Knowledge Base or Support Site

A knowledge base is another ideal use for a wiki, and if you've built product documentation on a wiki already, a knowledge base can be the logical next step. Keep common FAQs and support questions on the wiki so they can be easily updated with new information. People inside your organization can update it with new information like questions, issues, solutions, and how-to guides.

A wiki knowledge base can be especially useful for support staff so they can update it as soon as they find a new answer to a question, or add new issues in need of answers. Because the wiki tends to "pull" information from the edges of a group into a central place that everyone sees, it helps reveal information that people might not realize others have or are looking for. In the case of a support group, it helps bring to light the issues that need answers so someone who knows an answer can easily contribute it. With a constantly growing wiki knowledge base, support staff can answer questions a lot faster because it cuts down on the unnecessary repetition that happens when people are working in relative isolation and don't have a mechanism to share what they know.

Some organizations open the wiki knowledge base to customers so they can directly update it. As the wiki becomes more comprehensive and people increasingly look there first for simple issues, support staff has more time to concentrate on new and more specific issues. Customers can also directly support each other through the information they post to the wiki, and if the knowledge base includes a peer directory, they can discuss issues directly and work together to solve them, and then add new information to the knowledge base. Heck, this could even lead to those customers realizing they have complementary interests and collaborating on other projects!

Event Planning

Start off by planning the event agenda, logistics, and documents like the agenda, all on the wiki. You can even use the wiki to distribute the invitation — just put it together on a wiki page, then use email and your blog to announce the event and include a link to full details on the wiki. You can also gather RSVPs on the wiki — set up a page that people can edit to add their name to a list, or have them RSVP by leaving a comment on the invitation page.

If you have materials to distribute before or after the event, you can use the wiki for this, too. Create a page on which to host all materials, or you can link them from items on the agenda. One advantage of doing this: presenters can attach copies of their presentation slides and handouts by themselves, without having to email them to you. That's a great way to further cut down on unnecessary email, and you can still check the documents they add to the wiki and contact them if any changes are needed.

Intranet or Extranet

Use a wiki for your intranet or extranet. The problem with the traditional intranet is it doesn't encourage people to contribute often. One person is usually responsible for updating it, and when lots of changes have to be funneled through that person, information on the intranet gets out of date quickly.

Imagine the scenario — you ask the intranet person to make changes to a page, but he or she already has a long list of changes to make so yours takes days or weeks to happen. When you haven't seen the change, you probably email the person for an update, and if everyone else is doing that the person is even more distracted by answering those emails, so the change takes even longer. By the time the change is made, that information is already out of date and the cycle starts all over again. Or not. Eventually, you just stop asking for changes to the intranet because it's just too difficult and not useful.

At Atlassian, we use a wiki for the company extranet. Development teams, departments such as marketing, sales, and customer advocates each have a wiki space. The ability for logged in users to view content in different spaces across the extranet isn't restricted by default, but pages can be restricted as needed. Project documents, standard materials like company and product logos, meeting agendas and summaries, and draft content for the website and public blogs are all developed on the wiki. Some information is developed collaboratively, and some is developed individually, but because of the wiki it's well organized and easy to find, which makes content easy to use as needed.

Blogging

Some wiki tools have the ability to support blogging. At Atlassian, internal blogging is used to communicate about activities like product development, support issues, product releases, planning events such as user groups and conferences, and providing informal updates on miscellaneous issues like server updates. Because blogging takes place on the wiki, it adds further value to the wiki as a central information source, and is a better way to distribute information than further clogging people's email inboxes, because people can identify the information most relevant to them. When they do so, they're more likely to make a meaningful contribution than if they were just copied on lots of emails that someone else may have thought they'd be interested in.

Using internal blogging for routine updates and information allows email to be used only for updates that truly affect everyone and need to be communicated in a blanket manner. By reducing the number of general emails, people will be more likely to pay attention to the few that really do affect them, and by putting more specific communication on the wiki, people can identify and keep up with what's most relevant to them.

External Communication

A wiki can be used as a simple platform for internally editing content, then allowing an external audience to just read and comment on it, but not edit. For instance, you might use a wiki internally to collaboratively write news releases. You might start by asking for input from various internal groups working on a project for which public news is being released. Public relations and marketing staff would then draft a news release, ask appropriate parties to refine and vet the content, and then finalize the release. If something changes, the release can be quickly updated as necessary.

Once the release is ready to be released to the public, the wiki can be used for this as well. Most enterprise wiki software has the ability to set permissions regarding who can read and edit content, so the finished news release could be put on a wiki page where permissions are set to allow anyone to read, but only those who are logged in are allowed to modify the document. Members of the public could also be allowed to add comments to the page, which would still preclude them from editing the actual content, but would allow a mechanism for feedback, comments, and questions relating to the news. Staff could answer questions by posting reply comments, and because they would be logged in, their names would appear with their comments, indicating that they are official replies.

Public Website

Another use for the wiki is as the platform for a public website. The fact that it can be easily edited just makes the job of keeping content up to date much easier. This is not likely to be the first wiki use you might think of, but some of the ideas I suggested earlier are essentially public website uses of the wiki, such as a public support site or knowledge base.

Wikipatterns.com is an example of a wiki used as a public website. The first time you visit, it might not even be apparent that it's a wiki, but when you want to contribute to a pattern page, build a personal profile, or add a new pattern, the edit button is right there.

Last year, along with eight collaborators, I wrote the wikibook, *Using Wiki in Education* (wikiineducation.com), entirely on a wiki and even released it to readers on the wiki as well. Most chapters are read-only, but one is editable by general readers, as are some pages on the site where readers can contribute links to other wiki-related content.

And Many More!

These are just a few examples of how a wiki might be used in your organization, but the best part is, you'll think of many more and when you do, you'll be able to use the wiki! Also, although the wiki is an excellent collaboration tool, not all of the activities that take place on it must be collaborative — drafting blog posts for example — but the flexibility and lack of rigid structure means the wiki can be used for all these activities and the more you use it, the more valuable it becomes to everyone in your organization. The next chapter discusses how to get your wiki use underway and encourage people to make the all-important first edit.

References

Giles, Jim. "Internet encyclopedias go head-to-head," *Nature* 438, no. 7070 (14 December 2005), www.nature.com/news/2005/051212/full/438900a.html (accessed 16 May 2007).

Jeliffe, Rick. "An interesting offer: get paid to contribute to Wikipedia," O'Reilly XML Blog (22 January 2007), www.oreillynet.com/xml/blog/2007/01/an_interesting_offer.html (accessed 9 July 2007).

Nature. "Wiki's wild world," (Editorial) News@Nature 438, 890 (15 December 2005), www.nature.com/news/2005/051212/full/438890a.html (accessed 9 July 2007).

Udell, Jon. "Heavy metal umlaut: the movie," Jon's Radio (21 January 2005), http://weblog.infoworld.com/udell/gems/umlaut.html (accessed 9 July 2007).

Case Study: Johns Hopkins University

Johns Hopkins University
Baltimore, Maryland, USA
`www.jhu.edu`
A Conversation with Geoffrey Corb, IT Director, Student Information Systems
Type of organization: University
   Number of wiki users: about 500
   Founded in 1876, Johns Hopkins University became the first research university in the United States. Its aim was two-fold — to advance students' knowledge and to advance the general human knowledge through discovery and scholarship. Today, more than a century later, the University spans across nine academic and research divisions, each of which is grouped among the finest schools of the country. With its emphasis on learning and research, Johns Hopkins University has revolutionized higher education within the United States.

1. Why did you choose a wiki?

In the midst of implementing a sophisticated new student information system for the university, we found ourselves plagued with a number of problems not all that uncommon to large system implementation projects. First and foremost, we had and were continuing to develop significant knowledge about the product and system that we were implementing and needed someplace to store and organize it. In addition, document management was a challenge, with documents being stored in a number of places on the network and being constantly circulated via email. Finally, with constant activity on a project of this nature, project participants were becoming numb to the volume of emails being distributed by the project staff; we needed a better way to communicate with project participants and stakeholders. Though our project implementation was nearly half completed by the time we initially implemented our wiki, the wiki helped address these challenges and markedly improved performance and understanding of project participants.

2.   What type of wiki are you using?

We have implemented an enterprise wiki product. Due to the nature of the purpose of our wiki — to support the implementation of a mission-critical university system — it is not open to the general public, but it is open to all who have a legitimate need. Its use is expanding to include other initiatives; however it is still not publicly accessible.

3.   How are you using the wiki?

We are using the wiki for just about everything we do — it has become an extensive knowledge base for us. With very few exceptions, all of our project and department-related meetings are documented in our wiki, first by posting an agenda and later updated with the notes from the meeting. Staff members are blogging instead of completing weekly status reports. Key project documentation exists only in the wiki and now only as wiki content, not attached files. Specifications and artifacts generated through the development process are also created as wiki content and are progressively elaborated by a wide audience of contributors. We have recently started to migrate the online, context-sensitive help system from a static, generated website into the wiki to allow our users to help us maintain the documentation, document hints, tips, and workarounds, and use the commenting feature to have conversations with one another about system functionality. My department has created a departmental intranet in their own space; my management team has a space for managing our department's operations. Special projects or university-wide task forces use the wiki for collaboration among geographically-dispersed participants. There is truly little that we do that doesn't find its way into the wiki in some way, shape, or form.

4. Looking at `Wikipatterns.com`, what patterns are in use on your wiki?

These patterns were not defined when we first implemented our wiki, starting in late 2004. Retrospectively, it appears that we have employed the following patterns in our wiki: *Champion, Invitation, Maintainer, MySpace, StartingPoint, Viral, WikiGnome, WikiZenMaster, Agenda, ContentAlert, Magnet, Scaffold, Wiki Not Email.*

5. What changes have you seen as a result of using a wiki?

We have found that people involved in our projects are more well informed than ever before. Trust has strengthened between project participants and stakeholders since our operations are more transparent than ever before. We have dramatically reduced the number of emails that circulate with attachments; at the same time, dramatically increased the number of emails that circulate with links to wiki content. There is more collaboration between team members than ever before: People will quickly post an idea and others will promptly comment on the idea, elaborate the idea, sometimes invalidate the idea, and so on.

CHAPTER 3

What's Five Minutes Really Worth?

THAT'S WHY MICROSOFT SOFTWARE ASSURANCE IS SO IMPORTANT

Geek and Poke (http://geekandpoke.typepad.com).
Courtesy of Oliver Widder. Used with permission.

The chief difference between the wiki and more traditional content management (CM) or knowledge management (KM) systems is structure. Whereas most ECM and KM tools are built with defined structure in the form of processes, workflows, and architectures, the wiki starts off with the minimum possible structure and grows a custom structure based on how each person, team, department, or project uses it.

It's much easier at the outset to "sell" a tool — both in the financial and conceptual sense — that has defined structure, processes, and features because it can be presented as a solution for a specific need. It may do a good job meeting that specific need, but the tool runs into trouble when people inevitably try to apply it to other needs that may be very different from the initial need it was meant to meet. This is often the scenario in enterprises, and one of the main reasons why the promise of KM and CM systems hasn't been fully realized more than a decade after they initially appeared on the scene.

What Happened to Knowledge Management?

In "Whence goeth KM?" Dave Snowden (2006) concludes that knowledge management (KM) is on its way out because it has changed so much since it first appeared in the early 1990s. KM came to prominence at the same time that technology was beginning to emerge and dominate organizational thinking. "Most people forget that when KM started computing was still fairly new. The Internet was in its early stages, email was not yet universal and the sheer volume of information that is now available was hardly envisaged by other than an enlightened few" (Snowden 2006). People were starting to figure out how to use technology to gather, organize, and manage knowledge in a more collaborative, minimally structured way, but were still stuck working within the existing paradigm of hierarchy and tightly controlled access to information.

Because they were based on the prevailing thinking of the day, KM tools were designed to structure the knowledge process and allow people to maintain the hierarchical control they were accustomed to. Furthermore, they were also built to meet the needs of one type of user. "The big consultancies entered the field and built KM systems for people who spent their entire life writing reports, and then tried to move those systems sideways into very different organizations" (Snowden, 2006). This made it extremely difficult to reuse them in other areas, made content more difficult to access by anyone other than the users a system was designed for, and isolated users as they focused completely on learning processes and workflows in these systems.

Because of this emphasis on content, KM tools haven't focused on connecting people naturally with as few boundaries as possible. Human intelligence and behavior is pattern-based, but KM systems are centered around the workflow, that is, one person authors a document and others read and approve it in a linear fashion. This doesn't make sense in both a behavioral and practical context because it runs counter to natural patterns of human interaction. For example, what if you finished a document and sent it along the review and approval chain, and then remembered something critical that you wanted to add? Would you add it and start the whole review process again, or just forget it? When you need to add or edit content, you should be able to do so easily without any fear of disrupting a highly structured process.

Furthermore, those early KM systems tried to treat tacit knowledge (stored in peoples' heads) as something that could be extracted and turned into explicit knowledge (written down), and then turned back into tacit knowledge simply by another person reading it. The idea behind this approach was that peoples' knowledge could be fed into the system, and housed completely separate from the people themselves for reuse by others. "Early attempts at KM focused on removing dependency on people, 'extracting' their knowledge into databases and organizing it into neat and tidy taxonomies" (Snowden, 2006). The flaw here is that tacit knowledge is intimately connected to the person in whose head it is stored, and people need to directly communicate with each other to transfer both tacit knowledge and the context surrounding it.

Something Wiki This Way Comes

The wiki is a complete departure from the principles of highly managed knowledge creation. Unlike KM systems, wikis focus completely on letting people work together online the same way they'd work in person, and approach knowledge as the product of that organic, nonlinear human connection and collaboration. They deliberately leave out pre-built structure, complex procedures, workflows, and leave it up to the people using a wiki to define the ways they'll use it and how they'll organize their information. Ward Cunningham originally described the wiki as, "The simplest online database that could possibly work" (Cunningham, 2002).

This does make a wiki more challenging to explain, especially to skeptics. It doesn't just do one thing, and because people are used to thinking of software as having a specific use, it's sometimes harder at first for them to grasp the potential of the wiki.

Once people understand it, it's a much more valuable tool because the lack of rigid structure means it can be used to do almost anything people immediately think of. Over time, as people inevitably think of other uses, the wiki can handle them just as deftly. More rigid tools need a lot of tweaking and still won't perform functions beyond their original design in an elegant, efficient way that makes people's work easier. The wiki will do an elegant, efficient job because it is designed to do so in an intuitive way.

Taking the processes and structure out of the picture also makes the tool itself smaller, less technically complex and resource intensive, and more reliable. There's less to buy because you can have an enterprise wiki running on a single server that costs just a few thousand dollars. There's less that can go wrong with it because the underlying code base isn't as complex, and when problems do occur they can be fixed faster. There's also less to justify financially, because an enterprise wiki that can support hundreds of individual wiki spaces and thousands of users costs a small fraction of the price of content management and knowledge management systems.

What Makes a Wiki a Wiki?

Let's look at what's unique about the wiki, and why it's different from other collaboration and content management tools. In a general sense, a wiki does perform the functions of content management — creation, editing, organization, and storage — but it's *how* the wiki does these things that makes it unique.

Basic Structure

Beyond the legendary ease of editing, perhaps the most important principle of the wiki is its conscious emphasis on using as little structure as possible to get the job done, and nothing more. A wiki doesn't force hierarchy, and this flies in the face of tradition where content management systems rely on a predefined hierarchy to organize information, and content is organized and accessed within the confines of this hierarchy.

Instead, an individual wiki starts out flat, with all pages on an equal level. This allows people to create organization that makes the most sense for their work styles and the content they're working on. For example, if a team is using a wiki to organize their meetings and projects, they might maintain two lists on the homepage: one consisting of links to pages containing meeting agendas and minutes, and the other containing links to pages for managing each project.

The Enterprise Wiki: Spaces and Pages

A wiki is the equivalent of a single website, and an enterprise wiki enables simplified management of multiple wikis for groups, teams, and projects. This is where the concept of spaces comes in. With Confluence, for example, the overall wiki is called the *site*, such as `http://confluence.atlassian.com`. Within that site are *spaces* for different topics, groups, projects, and products. For example, if you were looking for information on plug-ins for Confluence, you would visit `http://confluence.atlassian.com` and choose the space called Confluence Extension. Inside that space, you would find a page for each plug-in with information including the author, version number, description, download link, and documentation. Spaces are simply individual wikis within the enterprise wiki framework. They're just like individual websites, and can even be accessed via their own specific addresses. For example, the Confluence Extension space URL is `http://confluence.atlassian.com/display/CONFEXT`.

What makes an enterprise wiki attractive to organizations is the single framework for managing multiple wikis. An enterprise wiki is easier to manage and scales with growing demand for wiki use because creating a new space is a matter of a few clicks instead of having to install a new wiki each time one is requested. With regard to user accounts and access to wikis, an enterprise wiki is better for organizations because each time a new space is created, people can use the same account to access multiple spaces, instead of having to remember multiple usernames and passwords.

Furthermore, an enterprise wiki can connect to an organization's existing Lightweight Directory Access Protocol (LDAP) repository, which contains the central database of user accounts for services such as email and network access, which means the wiki login can be the same username and password each person already knows and uses. The simplicity of being able to use the same account helps drive user adoption, because it removes the potential barrier of having to remember another account, and helps make the enterprise wiki part of the mainstream set of tools people use.

For users, an enterprise wiki makes it easier to keep abreast of activity in all the spaces in which she or he is involved, because pages can be added to a list of favorites for faster access and monitoring changes via email or an RSS feed. It's also easier to get a general sense of what's going on right when you log in. The first page you see is a dashboard that gives you a snapshot of the entire enterprise wiki with lists of all spaces you have access to, recently updated pages in those spaces, and pages you've marked as favorites. In addition you'll see a tool to create an RSS feed of pages and spaces you want to monitor, quick access to your personal space, and a link to start a blog post.

Features such as central management and creation of spaces, ability to manage access to spaces via a permission system, connections to other enterprise tools, and the ability for users to access the wiki easily using existing accounts are critical to satisfying organizations' requirements for a tool that is robust and secure enough to be part of their core infrastructure. For users, being able to use their existing username and password to access the wiki, monitor changes via email and RSS, and easily access multiple spaces are the kinds of features that make the wiki become an indispensable tool.

Editing Pages and Creating Content

A wiki makes creating content easy for people at all levels of technical knowledge. One of the hallmarks of wiki editing is wiki markup (Figure 3-1), a system of simple formatting prompts that is easier to learn than HTML code and faster than the toolbar and button based interfaces in word processing software.

For example, to make text bold using wiki markup, you'd just put asterisks at the beginning and end of the text you want to appear bold, *like this*.

Notation	Function
`*bold*`	makes text **bold**
`_italic_`	makes text *italic*
`-strikethrough-`	adds strikethrough to text
`+underlined+`	makes text <u>underlined</u>
`^superscript^`	creates ^{superscript} text
`~subscript~`	creates $_{subscript}$ text

`{quote}`
`Hello World!`
`{quote}`
	displays text in a blockquote

`[Link]`	links to another page with title "Link" within the same wiki space
`{anchor:anchorname}`	creates an anchor point within a wiki page
`[Link#anchor]`	links to an anchor within a page in the same wiki space
`[link alias|spacekey:pagetitle]`	links to a wiki page within another space in the enterprise wiki
`[link alias|spacekey:pagetitle#anchor]`	links to an anchor within a wiki page in another space
`[Wikipatterns.com|http://www.wikipatterns.com]`	Links to site outside the wiki, with syntax `[display text|website URL]`
`[mailto:stewart@atlassian.com]`	creates a link to an email address

`* bulleted`
`* list`
`** indented item`
`*** further indented item`
`* regular item`
	creates a bulleted list:
	  • bulleted
	  • list
	    ○ indented item
	      ▪ further indented item
	  • regular item

`# numbered`
`# list`
`## indented item`
`### further indented item`
`# regular item`
	creates a numbered list:
	  1. numbered
	  2. list
	    1. indented item
	      1. further indented item
	  3. regular item

`* bulleted`
`* list`
`*# nested numbered item`
`* regular item`
	nest a numbered item in a bulleted list:
	  • bulleted
	  • list
	    1. nested numbered item
	  • regular item

`# numbered`
`# list`
`#* nested bulleted item`
`# regular item`
	nest a bulleted item in a numbered list:
	  1. numbered
	  2. list
	    ○ nested bulleted item
	  3. regular item

Figure 3-1 Wiki markup used in Confluence

For italicized text, just put an underscore before and after_the text_. The idea behind wiki markup is to use such simple and intuitive notation that it's easy to remember and can be done right from your keyboard as you're typing.

I still remember my first encounter with wiki markup. For years I kept a simple to do list using just a Microsoft Word document open on one side of my display. In the document, I'd keep a sort of rudimentary bulleted list where the bullet point at the beginning of each line was simply an asterisk.

The first time I used a wiki, I created a bulleted list the exact same way and when I clicked "Save", the asterisks next to each list item became true bullet points. I said, "wow!" and it was immediately obvious to me how much thought had gone into making this system respond to the way people like me were already working.

As wikis have grown more popular and entered the mainstream, wiki vendors have added WYSIWYG (what you see is what you get) editors to make the editing experience look and feel more like the Microsoft Word-style interface many people are used to. The primary benefit of a WYSIWYG editor is that it can ease the transition when people first start using a wiki, but here's the rub: if it's the only editing tool people use, the WYSIWYG editor offers a much more limited editing experience and prevents people from making the leap necessary to fully understand the power of a wiki.

Once people get used to the wiki, using wiki markup at least some of the time makes editing more efficient because of its simplicity, ability to be added with just a few keystrokes when needed, and the range of formatting it enables.

Here's the HTML syntax for a standard hyperlink:

```
<a href=''http://www.wikipatterns.com'' >Visit
Wikipatterns.com</a>
```

Here's the same link in wiki markup:

[Visit Wikipatterns.com|www.wikipatterns.com]

Wiki markup is much simpler to write because it uses fewer characters to create the link. Creating the hyperlink using HTML required fourteen characters in addition to the web address (URL) and the display text, whereas wiki markup required only three. Also, in wiki markup the characters used are closer to natural writing. Placing brackets around the link is very similar to placing parentheses around text, and using a vertical bar to separate the display text and URL is the simplest way to format the two. Because people are so used to WYSIWYG editors and wiki markup has the word *"markup"* in its name, some people immediately assume it's in the same realm of complexity as HTML and are afraid to try it.

So what does this mean from the perspective of growing wiki adoption? Encourage people to use what's most comfortable, and educate them about wiki markup by emphasizing that it is a simple, quick shortcut for things such as making text bold and italic, creating hyperlinks, or building bulleted and numbered lists. Using a WYSIWYG editor is a good way to get started with wiki editing, but wiki markup offers some valuable formatting options and the advantage of speed and simplicity and the two editing options used together pack a powerful punch.

Folksonomy

Because wikis eschew strict hierarchy and formal structure, they allow for more evolutionary organization of content. Instead of one person arbitrarily deciding to put a file in a certain folder, such as on a shared drive, wikis allow people to tag pages with keywords describing their content. Tagging has emerged as one of the most effective ways to organize information because the organization is the result of a collaborative process where people create tags as needed to describe content, and instead of putting content in folders which is restrictive because a file can only reside in one folder, multiple tags can be assigned to a document by multiple people, which ultimately results in a better categorization of its content.

People can then search for individual tags, or combinations of tags, and wiki pages marked with those tags are returned. What does this mean for your enterprise wiki? Different teams, groups, and project wiki spaces can have pages on a particular topic, and as long as they are tagged with common tags, they can easily be found, yet they don't all have to be kept in the same place.

This kind of flexibility is one of the reasons why using a wiki improves collaboration. Those multiple teams working on different parts of a project previously had their content in multiple, disconnected places. One team was using email, another kept their documents on a shared drive, and a third had copies of documents scattered across peoples' computers. Now, thanks to the wiki and tagging, *all* the information can be accessed by anyone in those teams with just a simple search.

Recent Changes

With all this collaborative editing, how does a wiki keep track of changes to each page? Wikis maintain a revision history for every page that shows the time, date, author, and specific changes made with each revision. This allows people to see the progression of additions, changes, and deletions to a page. Additions are highlighted in green and deletions are highlighted in red so that you can quickly see where changes have been made to a page.

The revision history even allows you to revert a page back to an earlier version if necessary. Let's say you're working on a document and someone mistakenly deletes part of the contents of a wiki page. You can just access the revision history and restore the previous revision of the page with one click. What's interesting here is that whenever a change is made, the revision history records it as a new revision. So let's say the version of the wiki page with the partially deleted content is version 20, and you revert to version 19 to restore the deleted content. Instead of version 20 disappearing, a new version of the page is created. This new version 21 contains the same contents as version 19, but is a unique version of the page because it was created at a different time, and possibly by a different user. By doing this, the wiki creates an accurate picture of *all* changes to a wiki page, even deletions and restorations of the page itself.

Wikis let you keep track of changes using email and RSS notification systems. You can subscribe to an email or RSS feed that notifies you when a page has been changed, and gives you a quick snapshot of the changes. As your wiki use grows and you need to keep track of what's happening on an increasing number of pages, this is an important timesaver because it saves you from having to manually check all those pages.

It also allows you to make more timely contributions. Because you're notified as soon as someone else makes a change to a page, you can edit it or leave comments as soon as you receive notification as opposed to arbitrarily checking the page for changes and possibly contributing a while after the last edit. This helps maintain a frequency of editing that gets a collaborative task done faster and ensures that everyone involved is better informed about the process.

Balancing Trust and Control: Why Wikis Have Succeeded Where Others Have Failed

Wikis shift the social balance away from control and closer to trust. This is a fundamental difference because it democratizes information and collaboration on the principle that greater participation is ultimately better than control, and a fundamentally open system with provisions for control when necessary is better than a fundamentally closed system. There are two reasons for this: The first has to do with technology and the second has to do with people.

From an information architecture standpoint, software that's designed to impose a high level of control over access and content structure is more complex by design. It has to have the ability to maintain complex structures built into it, and this restricts its flexibility. This can make it difficult or even impossible for it to support a low level of structure, sometimes simply because it's too difficult for the average user to figure it out! The bottom line is it's much harder to have an open collaboration environment using a tool that's fundamentally designed to be closed.

On the other hand, the wiki is designed the opposite way. The simplest configuration of a wiki is for it to be completely open: Anyone can read, and anyone can edit. This keeps complexity to a minimum from an architectural standpoint — the software is simpler and less prone to errors because less can go wrong. It also means the wiki can be used for a wider range of needs, and people can learn how to use it faster so they're getting to productive uses of it faster than if they were using more complex tools where they have to learn a specific, often complex procedure for each new task.

On top of this lean foundation, enterprise wiki software includes permission capability that allows viewing and editing privileges in different spaces in a wiki to be restricted when needed. For instance, on `Wikipatterns.com` the public site resides in a space where viewing is open to anyone who visits, and editing is open to all registered users. Registration is free and required because it builds a stronger community where each member is personally accountable for his or her edits because his or her name is associated with them. The homepage has slightly different permissions. Anyone can view it, but editing is restricted to just two site administrator accounts because there isn't really anything the user would edit on the homepage, and you want to maintain a consistent look and feel at the entrance to the wiki.

Besides the public space, I'm using a private space to write this book. Using the permission system, I restricted access to just my editor's account and my own, so that we could work together on the manuscript. As I write each chapter, drafts are immediately available for her to read and leave feedback. She can either edit the page itself and put suggestions or corrections at exact points in the draft, or leave general comments at the bottom of any page. This saves an incredible amount of time because we don't have to send attachments back and forth by email. When she leaves me suggestions, I can act on them immediately, and she can see the results just as quickly.

Now that we've looked at the technical reasons why it's easier to use a fundamentally open system like a wiki, let's take a look at the social reasons. Closed systems implicitly assume that people can't be trusted and technology has to be relied on to control access to information. This encourages an organizational culture where people don't trust each other and are concerned with maintaining control over information access. Some people do this because of the perception that with control comes power, and they don't want to give up that power. Others operate on the perception that they should keep information close to the vest so they'll be perceived as experts and others will need to come to them for information, thus safeguarding their position. The closed approach creates inefficiency, information redundancy, and reduced focus on common goals because it's hard for people to know what others are doing so information ends up in restricted silos, and it is difficult to change this behavior once it becomes ingrained.

Fundamentally open tools such as the wiki encourage just the opposite. Their design assumes that people can be trusted with the information they have access to, and will use it responsibly to further shared goals. This encourages a culture where people do trust each other, and involve others in their work to build the best possible end product in less time and with less unnecessary back and forth effort. This also reduces redundancy because people can build and collectively maintain shared information sources.

It also does away with that antiquated idea that a person has to hoard information to protect their position and be perceived as an expert. In a wiki-based organizational culture, people are rewarded by how much they actively contribute to the community. Those who share more generally become the thought leaders because their expertise can be tangibly measured by their contributions and their approachability. These people become truly indispensable to an organization because not only do they have a wealth of information, but more importantly they're willing to share it.

The value of information is in direct proportion to the number of people that can use it, and wikis enhance this value by unlocking previously hidden or inaccessible information and giving people the ability to better use it and keep it up to date.

How Atlassian Uses a Wiki to Increase Transparency and Decrease Distance

At Atlassian, we use Confluence — our enterprise wiki — for the company extranet. Every team, product, and project has a wiki space and everyone within the company has access to all spaces. Each person also has a personal wiki space he or she can use to post a picture, biography, contact information like phone, email, and IM, links to favorite websites, and so on. Morgan Friberg, a Customer Advocate, describes it this way: "One of the first tasks for new employees is to create a personal space and add information about yourself. Once employees do this and realize the extranet is the lifeblood of Atlassian, it is much easier to access information and add content to the internal wiki. Before long, I was blogging, creating new pages, adding comments, and cleaning up Atlassian's extranet every single day I work!"

People also use their personal spaces to blog about progress on various projects, technology and industry developments, useful links, and whatever else they deem worthy. Blog posts are an excellent way to communicate relevant information, spur conversations and debate, and get feedback on ideas, issues, and projects.

This is especially important because the company is spread across three cities on different continents. Atlassian's headquarters are in Sydney, Australia, and it has offices in San Francisco, California (U.S.), and Kuala Lumpur, Malaysia. With time differences of as much as 17 hours, the wiki makes it possible for a person in the Sydney office to work on a project, update information, or blog about a topic, and people in the San Francisco office can contribute, comment, or collaborate during their working hours, while the person in Sydney is asleep!

Giving all employees the ability to access all spaces encourages everyone to be as transparent as possible about how they work, and to keep their work well organized so that others can easily find what they need and use it. The time difference makes transparency important because it's not always possible for a person in one office to just call a person in another office on a moment's notice. For example, when it's mid-afternoon in Kuala Lumpur, it's late at night in San Francisco.

Beyond these reasons why using a wiki is beneficial for a global company like Atlassian, there are some other benefits. When I traveled to the Sydney office for the first time in July 2007, I met several people in person for the first time, but I felt like I already knew them from seeing their pictures and biographies in their personal spaces, commenting on their blog posts (and getting their feedback on mine), and collaborating with them on several projects using the wiki.

This is the kind of benefit that's directly contributing to the more traditional business benefits because it closes the otherwise large organizational, social, and cultural gap that exists when people are halfway around the world from each other. At Atlassian, that gap is minimized by the fact that the wiki is the central hub of activity.

User-generated Templates

Content management systems have specific, often highly structured and rigid templates for different types of content that users can't easily change. A wiki, by contrast, allows you to build the structure that best suits your content. Later on, you can use that structure to create a simple template that can be applied to other pages as they are created.

For example, when I advise a team to use a wiki to manage meeting agendas and minutes, I suggest that they build a basic structure for an agenda page (Figure 3-2) that includes meeting date, attendees, items to address and the name of the person who submitted each item, and anything else they want as part of the agenda.

Once the structure for the page is essentially complete, I show them how to make that structure into a simple template so that each time they add a new page for a meeting they have the option of applying that template. Unlike rigid templates, all the wiki template does is put the basic headings and empty list onto the new page, so they just have to fill in the agenda items, date, attendees, and other information. And if they want to change the page after they've added the template, they can just remove what they don't need right from the page.

This kind of flexible, user-generated template system is better than using rigid, pre-created templates because it allows people to go beyond just organizing their information. It enables teams to look at how they work, and make adjustments to be more productive. Best of all, that improved efficiency is

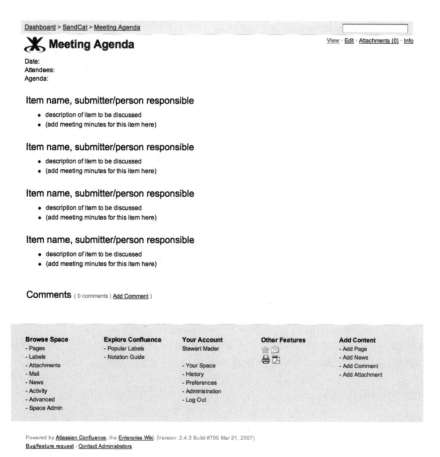

Figure 3-2 An example meeting template

the result of a collaborative process, and can actually make people feel more satisfied with the way they spend time.

One team I worked with was having trouble keeping weekly meetings within the planned time, and often had to schedule a second meeting later in each week to cover topics they didn't get to in the regularly scheduled meeting. To fix this, they decided to use the wiki-based agenda to keep track of how much time they spent on each item during meetings, so they could better plan future meetings. They added a prompt in their template to record the time spent, and looked at which types of topics took up the most time.

Equipped with this information, they now schedule meetings with the most time-intensive topics covered every other week instead of every week, and they also schedule some topics for virtual-only discussion, which takes place right on the wiki page for each meeting. Both of these approaches have resulted in fewer scheduled meetings running over time, and fewer "unscheduled" meetings to deal with the overflow of topics. By using the wiki to manage meetings, they were able to see where time management was inefficient and improve it with a mix of better scheduling and virtually meeting on the wiki. Both approaches ease people's schedules by eliminating time spent in extra meetings and tapping into the time people already spend online.

Extending Wikis

Wikis balance simplicity and customization by allowing users to develop plug-ins to perform specific tasks. This is a smarter approach than trying to make it do everything for everyone and ending up with a tool that doesn't do anything really well. It's impossible for a software vendor to please everybody, and it's not a good business decision to do so, because the vendor should be focused on building an amazing, high-quality core product. The challenge for every software maker is prioritizing how it allocates its development resources, and if it tries to please everyone it will be spread too thin, overall quality will suffer, all the custom requests will still take a long time to fulfill, and nobody will be pleased anyway.

Providing the capability to build plug-ins in lieu of building lots of features allows a more compact, highly focused development team to make a responsive, powerful, scalable core platform. That strong platform provides the basis for a community to build an ecosystem of plug-ins and added functionality that itself is scalable and can be more comprehensive than if the software maker tried to satisfy everyone. For those using the wiki, the plug-in ecosystem is a lot faster and ultimately less expensive than waiting for a software maker to build a new feature, because they can rely on the community to find an existing plug-in that meets their needs, or find someone who specializes in building plug-ins for the software. This keeps wikis simple and reliable at the core, but customizable when necessary to meet specific needs.

Back-office to Front-office

The wiki has risen to mainstream recognition and use in part because it fits very well with some of the key characteristics of the Web 2.0 phenomenon. Like many Web 2.0 tools, it puts more emphasis on intuitive design and usability than a constantly growing feature list. It also aims for the simplest way to perform its main tasks, and social interaction is at the core of how it functions.

Because the first wikis were created to respond to software development needs, they were largely back-office tools from their creation in the mid-1990s to the early part of this decade. Developers use them to track development of their software projects and products, collaboratively write documentation, and quickly share content, such as code snippets. IT staff use them to track projects, document solutions to hardware and software issues, publish online documentation for the tools and services they support, and make information more easily searchable by conducting conversations on the wiki instead of over email.

For this reason, when organizations consider using the wiki as a business tool for the whole enterprise, they often find that they already have a wiki, and their IT staff is already very knowledgeable about the tool itself and how to use a wiki in combination with other tools like email and traditional content management tools.

Let's look at three examples of how the wiki compares to other tools: email, intranet, and shared drives. The bottom line in each case is that the wiki shouldn't be a wholesale replacement for these tools, but it does perform specific tasks better than these other tools, and can free the others to be better used for their strengths.

Wiki versus Email

The primary difference between using a wiki and email for collaboration is in the mechanics of each. If you and I were using email and a text document to collaborate, a lot would have to happen between when I edit the document and when you can edit it. Once I'm finished editing I have to save changes to the file, then create an email, address it to you, write a message, attach the file, and send it. Then you wait for the email to arrive in your inbox, which may happen quickly or take some time depending on circumstances outside of our control, like network traffic and virus scanning by the email server.

Once you receive the email, you have to open it and download the attachment. Right here there's the issue of viruses in email attachments. Although I wouldn't intentionally send you one, so many viruses have been spread through email that the whole notion of attachments is a touchy issue for people. In fact, many organizations limit what file types you can send as attachments, and some even ban attachments altogether! Once you download it, you have to open it. Hopefully you have the right software, and version of that software, to open my document. Next to the concern over viruses, this is one of the biggest headaches in collaboration because having the wrong version may mean you can't open the file at all, and in some cases trying to edit a file with several different versions of a software application can wreak havoc on the document's formatting. Whew! Finally, after all that mechanical work, you can finally contribute to that document.

But wait! What happens if I send you that document, *then* get a great idea for something to add? Should I wait until you've had time to look over and possibly edit the file to send my new idea? This isn't so good because my addition may be time sensitive and need to be added at this moment, or it may fundamentally improve the content of the document. If I wait to edit the document until you've edited it, I might forget my idea.

So waiting isn't a good idea. In that case, should I send along an updated version with my new idea? The risk here is that by the time you receive the second document you might have already started editing the first one, and now the progression of content construction has forked into two separate threads, and you'll have to manually reconcile the two files to make sure your edits get into the file with my most recent edits. If you haven't started editing yet and have the two documents in your inbox, there's a risk you might not see the new one, might not know which one to edit and pick at random, or think the new one is just a duplicate email. Here again, you might choose the earlier one by mistake. This results in the same situation where one of us has to reconcile edits between the two documents, and who wants to do that?

If we were using a wiki in that same scenario, almost all the mechanics between when you and I edit the document have been removed, and you could see my changes to the document as soon as I save the wiki page. Now, if I get that great idea a few minutes after I've saved the page, I just click edit, contribute my idea, and as soon as I click "Save" you'll have the most recent document instantly available.

Keep in mind that I've just given the simplest example with only two people. If it can be this difficult for only two people to "collaborate" over email, imagine how these problems can balloon exponentially when more people are involved! A new wiki user recently told me a story of how it took three days to reconcile the edits that had gotten out of control when twelve people tried to use email to collaborate on a press release. The edits themselves didn't take that long — within a few hours after the file had been emailed to everyone, twelve distinct files were returned with twelve different sets of edits!

If they had used a wiki, *everything* would have been done within those few hours. Edits would have taken place on the same "canvas," and as each person visited the wiki to review the release and add their input, they would have seen the most up-to-date version of the content with the latest edits incorporated. Each time a person edited the page, changes would be based on the current state of the content, instead of the original, unedited state, as was the case with each person working in isolation on a separate copy of the emailed document. The wiki could also notify people via email or RSS feed each time the document was changed, which could prompt them to make further changes if they saw an edit and thought to add or edit something further.

In the end, the press release would have taken less time to create and refine, and the process to get to the final product would have better reflected the interaction if these twelve people held an in-person meeting. That's what makes a wiki so special; it enables the natural patterns of interaction that previously could only happen in a physical meeting — fast-paced discussion, overlapping ideas, quick decisions on changes, quick error correction, introducing different viewpoints and collaboratively working to reach agreement — but it removes the need for everyone to be in the same place at the same time, and it documents the interaction better than a traditional meeting could.

What's Five Minutes Really Worth Anyway?

Let's say it's 2:55 P.M. and you have a meeting at 3:00 P.M. If we were collaborating with email and documents, you might see that message with the attached document and put it off until later because you don't have time to download and open the attachment, never mind make changes, before that 3:00 P.M. meeting. In this scenario I have to wait longer for your input, and if that meeting lasts a long time, you might not even be able to make changes to document until the next day.

By contrast, if we were using a wiki, you might see the wiki page at 2:55 P.M. waiting for your input, and decide to give it a quick read. If you get a great idea, want to make some minor changes, or even just notice a typo, all you have to do is click "Edit", make some quick changes, click "Save", and head off to your meeting. Now that the document has your input, collaboration can keep moving forward because I can revise based on your edits, send it to others for further input, and so on.

Because of the wiki, that five minutes between meetings just became much more productive than ever. Now multiply that increase in efficiency by all the press releases, meeting agendas, projects, reports, statistics, sales figures, business processes, and other documents that need this kind of input. Your organization can save hundreds — even thousands — of hours that right now are used inefficiently to reconcile the separate changes made to documents as a result of emailing them. Teams can shorten the time it takes to finish a project or product, which means getting it to market faster and increasing your competitive advantage. People can keep critical documents more up to date, which translates to fewer problems as a result of decisions made based on out-of-date information or business processes.

That's the difference a wiki can make for collaboration, and doing this can free up email and help diminish the stigma that's grown to surround email as a result of peoples' swelling inboxes. When organizations move collaboration over to the wiki, they reduce the awful congestion that results when a dozen people are copied on an email and most or all of them reply, and return email to its optimal use as a communication tool for more formal messages, and notifications. In fact, one great way to use email is to let a group of people know about the new wiki page you've created for collaboration!

Wiki versus Intranet Powered by Content Management System

The term *"intranet"* can refer to the internal network within an organization that is accessible only to employees or other authorized users, or the most visible part of that network, which is the website people use to access information. The intranet I refer to in this section is the latter, specifically when it is powered by a traditional content management system.

Have you ever used (or tried to use) an intranet and found out that the information you needed was out of date, or just wasn't there at all? That's because many intranets are set up with the good intention of providing an internal information source, but are too difficult to update or take too long because people can't directly update pages and instead have to funnel changes through a designated "gatekeeper."

Here's the scenario that often derails intranets: You want to update a page, but you can't directly edit it yourself. You have to find the person designated to update the intranet, and send your content to them. Because you can't just make that edit yourself and quickly cross it off your to do list, you lose that sense of accomplishment. So you put off the task until later, when you have a more significant number of updates, and can feel less like you're bothering that one overworked person who has to handle everybody's updates.

The consequence here is that information falls out of date as you wait longer to submit updates. Since that person designated to manage the intranet is often overwhelmed with updates, they are working through a backlog, which means that even when you do submit your updates they take a while to appear on the intranet. Because of this, information on the intranet grows stale, and people end up just emailing you when they need more current information.

When intranets are first introduced in organizations, there's a push to use them, and an initial flurry of activity. This initial popularity, combined with the bottleneck of only a few "gatekeepers" designated to update it, causes the backlog of updates that eventually slows the intranet to a crawl and results in out of date information. Since people can't just go in and update as needed, the intranet has very little "stickiness" with most employees, so it can't build the critical mass of users needed to be successful, and this is what causes intranets to fail.

By contrast, a wiki doesn't have this bottleneck so people can just fix or update something themselves, and they can do it immediately. Direct interaction with the wiki keeps it on peoples' minds and results in greater participation, which makes it more valuable. Also, because the best way to introduce a wiki is a grassroots approach, people who use it are more intrinsically motivated to do so, and will encourage their peers to do so as well. This builds a social network and support system that helps maintain the wiki's stickiness with users over a long period of time.

Wiki versus Shared Drive

The primary differences between using a wiki and using a shared drive for collaboration are access and version tracking. Some teams use shared drives to store files that multiple people need to access and edit, but they're often only in scattered use throughout organizations because they are not very scalable. The groups that use them successfully often are comprised of tech savvy people who understand the concept of network shared drives, know how to access them, and will put in the manual effort necessary to keep files organized.

But try to spread shared drives beyond these types of groups, and they are hard for the less tech savvy person to use. For the mainstream user, finding the right shared drive on the network can be challenging, which can lead to the scenario where people access the shared drive once, download copies of the files they need, then forget how to or find it difficult to get there again. The consequences here are files on the shared drive fall out of date, and there are numerous local copies of each file on peoples' computers — all being updated separately.

Even if people do try to keep files on the shared drive up to date, it's still difficult to manage different versions because it has to be done manually. When someone downloads a file and updates it, they also have to remember to update the file name with a new version number, and if someone forgets to do this, or uses the wrong version number, it can throw off versions for everyone else.

Simultaneous editing also presents a challenge. Let's say two people download version 15 of a file from the shared drive and update it at the same time. One person finishes first, changes the file name to version 16, and uploads it. What happens if the second person also names their file version 16, uploads it, and accidentally overwrites the version 16 that was just uploaded by the first person? Now changes are lost, and the person who uploaded the first version 16 has to download the second version 16 and add their changes to it.

Confused yet? Me, too.

Here's another scenario: What if the second person who downloaded version 15 of the file and edited it forgets to upload it? Meanwhile, others download, edit and upload the file several times. Now, the local copy of the file on that person's computer is further and further out of date, which means two things:

1. They're working with out of date information, which may poorly inform decisions.

2. Once they realize they're using an out of date version of the file, they have to work all of their local edits into the shared version of the file *and* learn all the new information they they've missed as the shared file has been updated.

Not fun.

This is where a wiki comes in. Web-based access is a much easier means to find information than hunting through network shared drives. Automatic version control means everyone is working with the most up-to-date version of content, and a notification system when someone else is editing means edits are much less likely to be overwritten.

Eliminating local editing means it's much easier to see the progression of information growth and change over time. With a shared drive scenario, this would require a lot of manual work to gather lots of different versions of files, but with a wiki versions can be compared side by side on a moment's notice. Also, notification by email or RSS whenever someone edits a page means other people can keep apprised of changes to the information they use every day, and can make decisions based on the most up-to-date information possible.

This is one of the reasons why most of what's written about wikis deals with social and organizational issues like appropriate behavior, where and how to use it, and so forth, instead of focusing on technical issues like just simply getting the thing working! Because it's so simple and intuitive, people are able to use it faster than most other tools. This is a unique phenomenon because the complexity, scope, and steep learning curves of other tools mean that learning about effective use happens much later, often long after people are using the tools in not so effective or efficient ways.

References

Cunningham, Ward. "What Is Wiki," www.wiki.org/wiki.cgi?WhatIsWiki, 27 June 2002 (Retrieved 25 July 2007).

Snowden, Dave. "Whence goeth KM?," www.cognitive-edge.com/2006/11/whence_goeth_km.php 21 November 2006 (Retrieved 25 July 2007).

Case Study: Sun Microsystems

Sun Microsystems, Inc.
Santa Clara, California, USA
`http://wikis.sun.com`
A Conversation with Linda Skrocki, Sr. Engineering Program Manager: Blogs, Forums, Planets, Wikis
Type of organization: High-tech company
Number of wiki users: 600+ at the end of the first month of the site being live
Sun Microsystems Inc., (NASDAQ: JAVA) provides network computing infrastructure solutions that include computer systems, software, storage, and services. Its core brands include the Java technology platform, the Solaris operating system, StorageTek, and the UltraSPARC processor.

1. Why did you choose a wiki?

Employees and Sun affiliates asked for a platform in which they can share and collaboratively create content based on common interests/initiatives. The wiki is open to people both inside and outside Sun. For example, a developer who is an advocate of Java but has never bought a Sun product could contribute to the wiki as long as they have a Sun online account and have been granted write access to the space by the space administrator.

2. What type of wiki are you using?

Enterprise, dual-node implementation outside of the firewall. Content is readable by anyone with a browser and writable by Sun employees, interns, and invited guests with a Sun online account (`https://reg.sun.com/register`).

By default, Sun employees have write access to the entire site, while external users have limited write access only within the spaces to which they've been granted access. Each space has a space administrator who can grant anyone write access to the space.

3. How are you using the wiki?

Collaboratively created documentation is a primary use for the wiki, with many spaces for specific initiatives dedicated to building and maintaining community created content.

Not all spaces are entirely Sun-centric, and that's as it should be. For the wiki to be successful, information should be on topics of interest to all participants. This increases the time people spend utilizing tools like blogs and wikis, which builds value as they engage with the tools, builds relationships, and humanizes the experience.

4. Looking at `Wikipatterns.com`, what patterns are in use on your wiki?

- **IdentityMatters:**   Sun requires that each contributor to the wiki have a Sun online account. This helps ensure that people make high-quality contributions, reduces the likelihood of anti-patterns like Vandalism or Trolling, and helps people value their interactions on the wiki just as they would in real life.

- **Poker:**   By giving wiki users the flexibility to create spaces that are not just Sun-centric, the company is encouraging people to build relationships and collaboratively create content. This builds a sense of ownership in the wiki, and increases the probability that people will use the wiki for all information that they consider important, including work-related content.

5. What changes have you seen as a result of using a wiki?

The site has only been live since August 3, 2007, but in that time about a thousand pages have been created by more than 600 users. As an example, the subject matter varies from general topics, such as social networking (`http://wikis.sun.com/display/SocialNetworking/Home`) to specific topics, such as FOSS Open Hardware Documentation (`http://wikis.sun.com/display/FOSSdocs/Home`).

11 Steps to a Successful Wiki Pilot

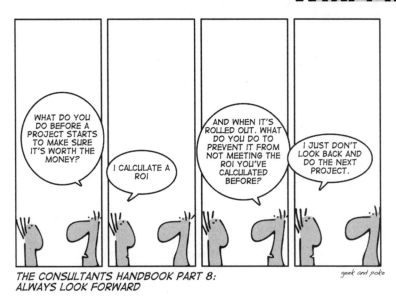

THE CONSULTANTS HANDBOOK PART 8:
ALWAYS LOOK FORWARD

geek and poke

Geek and Poke (http://geekandpoke.typepad.com). Courtesy of Oliver Widder.
Used with permission.

The first major step in making the wiki a core collaboration tool in your organization is to run a pilot. Every successful enterprise wiki rollout I've run or advised began with a pilot involving a small number of groups that are representative of the most common functions of the organization. The pilot is important because it allows you to get wiki use started in a controlled environment, build examples that are extremely relevant to your organization, and develop the administrative and support structure that will keep things running smoothly when the wiki is a full production service. It also lets you work out the kinks that are inevitable with a major software project.

The growth of the iPod is an excellent example of the benefits of a controlled rollout. Today, you see the iconic white headphones everywhere you go, but the iPod has reached this status through a steady and well-managed rise instead of an overnight explosion.

When the iPod was first launched in 2001, there was just one model, and it only worked with the Mac — think of this as the pilot phase. In fact, in an interview with *Newsweek*'s Steven Levy in October 2006, Apple CEO Steve Jobs explained how the Mac's small market share relative to PCs was used as leverage with the recording industry:

> Levy: 'Let's talk about the iTunes store. How did you get the record labels, which had been resisting digital music, to sign up?'
>
> Jobs: 'Now, remember, it was initially just on the Mac, so one of the arguments that we used was, "If we're completely wrong and you completely screw up the entire music market for Mac owners, the sandbox is small enough that you really won't damage the overall music industry very much." Then about six months later we were able to successfully persuade them to take down the barriers and let us move it out to the whole market' (Levy, 2006).

This is the quintessential rationale for a pilot project to test something new before spreading it everywhere. Testing with a small subset of users — in this case by restricting iTunes to just Mac users — Apple was able to test the market for legally downloaded music. This pilot gave it both the experience necessary to expand its online presence to PC users, and the evidence to convince record labels that consumers would buy fairly priced and easily accessible digital music as an alternative to piracy.

This same argument holds true in organizations, where people need to see the value of a tool before they will adopt it *en masse*. Because the wiki represents a big change in how people gather and organize information, and collaborate, a pilot project gives you the experience necessary to expand the wiki's presence throughout your organization, and the evidence necessary to convince skeptical users, inform pragmatic users, and inspire the early adopters to help you spread the word.

11 Steps to a Successful Pilot

Here are eleven steps for running a successful pilot. Some of this advice is intended for you to directly use and some is intended for you to give to people within pilot groups.

1. Establish a Time Frame

Set a reasonable time frame for groups to get familiar with the wiki, move the work relating to their pilot goal onto it, and reach the goal they set at the beginning of the pilot. Roughly three months is adequate — a fiscal quarter in business or a semester in educational institutions. The entire pilot, including setting up the wiki, technical integration with other enterprise services like LDAP directory for accounts, and testing will take approximately six months.

Keep in mind that this may take a longer or shorter amount of time depending on several factors, including the size of your organization and general attitudes toward using new tools. I've seen some groups take to the wiki in a week, and others take several months just to get started.

2.   Make It Representative

Include groups that are representative of typical projects and activities within your organization, so that you can build relevant examples and replicable strategies that can help when you expand wiki use to other groups later on. This makes wiki use more attractive to these groups because they can see directly relevant examples where other groups have found success using the wiki.

During the pilot, it gives you an opportunity to see how a cross section of groups in your organization use the wiki, and help them get the most value from using it.

3.   Keep It Compact

Keep your pilot size small enough that you can work closely with each pilot group. This allows you to have a remarkable command of the types of activities, which you can use whenever you need to report on the progress of the pilot. Keeping in close contact with pilot users enables you to quickly respond to potential problems as early as possible, and give groups timely guidance.

4.   Choose Participants Carefully

Make sure to include multiple types of users in the pilot. For the pilot to be useful later on when you expand wiki use to the whole organization, it has to show potential users a fully representative microcosm of wiki use in your organization, where people of all types can see themselves using the wiki.

Including only early adopters and tech savvy users won't just limit the appeal of the wiki to mainstream users; it will also limit your exposure to the types of issues common to the majority of future users. Include early adopters, but also be sure to include some people who are open to the technology but need to see its value demonstrated to fully commit to it, some thought leaders whose opinions will be more highly regarded (sometimes specifically because they're not early adopters!), and some skeptics. There's nothing better than having a former skeptic tell others how she or he has directly felt the positive impact of the wiki and is now an enthusiastic supporter!

5. Seek or Be Sought?

Should you advertise for participants in your pilot or hand pick them? This depends on the culture of your organization. In a tech savvy organization people may already know about the wiki, so putting out a call for participation will give you a pool of applicants from which to choose.

In an organization where people are comfortable with the technology they regularly use but don't necessarily follow the latest tech trends, it's better to hand pick some groups that you know would be receptive to trying new technology, but would approach it from a pragmatic perspective and be able to use their positive experiences to convince skeptical users later on.

6. Wiki with a Purpose

The wiki is no different than any other tool in that it must have a purpose to be successful. If you just show people the mechanics of editing a wiki page, they're not likely to become regular wiki users because they won't know how it relates to what they already do. If you've ever sat through any kind of technology training that only focuses on the tool itself, then you know what I'm talking about. You can't teach someone how to make an image by starting with a tutorial on Photoshop; you've got to start by asking what they want to include in the image, finding source material, and *then* putting it all together in Photoshop.

The wiki will have the greatest impact when used in response to specific *pain points* where knowledge construction and collaboration are not efficient. Once you know where it's needed, the best way to start is to get everyone together who will be using a wiki and have a conversation to mutually agree on how it will be used, and establish it as part of the existing social structure of your group, team, or project.

This is so important because it ensures that people see the wiki as a tool that helps them meet common needs, and see use of it as an activity everyone is welcome to — and should — participate in. One problem that has hindered earlier, more complex tools is the perception that they're just for "techies" or early adopters. The biggest strength of the wiki is that it isn't just for the most technically savvy groups, and has the highest probability of success when the greatest number of people buy into it and actively participate.

7. Define House Rules

Define a basic set of guidelines for content, conduct, and community and post them prominently on the wiki. You can use these guidelines as the basis to develop a more detailed wiki use policy for large-scale adoption. The next chapter covers this in more detail.

The Sony Ericsson Developer World Wiki has an excellent set of house rules that are concise, informative, and posted prominently on the homepage (`http://developer.sonyericsson.com/wiki`). Regarding community and conduct, they urge contributors to make constructive edits that are on topic, cite sources, respect others, be responsible, and use good judgment. Regarding content, they advise contributors to regard information on the wiki as constantly changing and shouldn't be taken as official, and that English is the official language in which contributions should be written.

8. Personal Spaces

Get spaces set up for the groups and have them get familiar with the wiki by creating Personal Spaces. A Personal Space (Figure 4-1) gives each user a place to post:

- Contact information: email, phone, IM — AIM, Yahoo, Google Talk, Skype, and so on
- Blog and personal website URL
- Biography

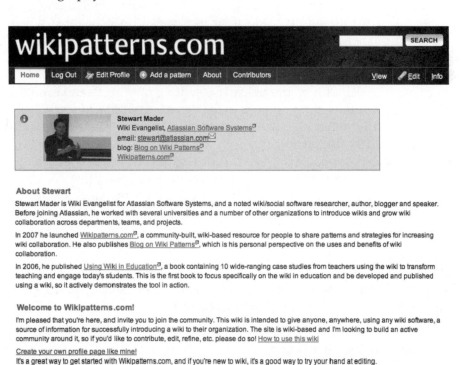

Figure 4-1 My personal space on `Wikipatterns.com`

Encourage blogging in personal spaces; this can be a good way for people to get to know more about each other and build community in teams, as well as a good place to update progress on projects, get informal feedback via comments, and float ideas.

Personal spaces build the social foundation of the wiki and give people a place to get comfortable with editing pages. Once groups start to work in their project spaces, this page editing experience will make it much easier for them to focus on getting used to collaborative editing, where they will change content someone else wrote or see content they wrote changed by someone else.

If someone is completely new to wiki editing, learning the mechanics of editing *and* grappling with the notion that content can be changed so quickly and collaboratively can be overwhelming. If they have editing experience, they will feel much more confident about engaging in the back-and-forth revision process that is central to the wiki and results in higher quality, more well-rounded information.

Once people are comfortable using the wiki, you can help them explore how to apply it to their work. Discuss projects, tasks, knowledge for critical processes, and so on that could make use of the wiki. Find out what's most important for the group to do their jobs well, and if possible where they feel information flow, collaboration, and so on is weak. This gives you specific instances to demonstrate how the wiki can meet their most important needs.

For example, a department might start by putting meeting agendas on the wiki before each staff meeting. Anyone in the department can add a new item, add additional information about an existing item, or delete something that's no longer relevant to the meeting.

During the meeting, people can take notes as items are discussed, effectively taking meeting minutes right on the wiki. From here, items that turn into projects or initiatives can be given their own space on the wiki for project management and collaboration, and the wiki becomes a *Magnet* for all manner of collaborative work.

NOTE More on this pattern: www.wikipatterns.com/MySpace

Contributors to this pattern on Wikipatterns.com **: lukehe, Sunir Shah, Trevor Pike, wikifirst, Remi Bachelet, Ronja Addams-Moring**

9. Never an Empty Page

As people set up new pages, encourage them to create a *Scaffold*, or template to guide others on what to put on each page. The scaffold can be as simple as a set of section headings, or it can be a set of brief guidelines so people can see

Figure 4-2 A sample scaffold

what types of information to include. Figure 4-2 shows a sample scaffold for a meeting agenda and minutes page:

On `Wikipatterns.com`, we use the scaffold pattern for all pattern pages (Figure 4-3):

NOTE More on this pattern: `www.wikipatterns.com/Scaffold`

Contributors to this pattern on `Wikipatterns.com`: **Laurent Peirone, Trevor Pike**

10. Make It a Magnet

When someone asks for information that you know is on the wiki, email a link to the appropriate wiki page. This helps people get in the habit of looking at the wiki, and increases the value of the wiki to each person because they can collaborate with more people via the wiki than email.

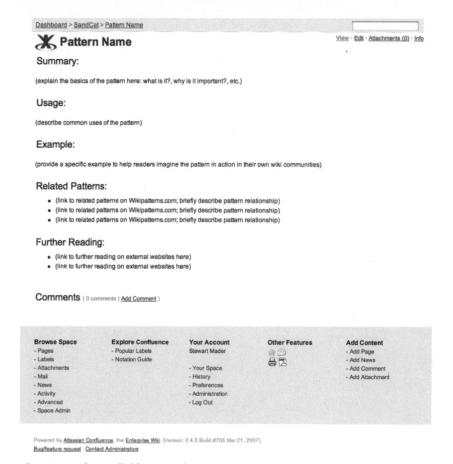

Figure 4-3 The scaffold pattern for `Wikipatterns.com`

It's also a good idea to put some exclusive content on the wiki so people get used to looking there. Pretty soon, ''It's on the wiki'' will become the default answer whenever people ask for information.

NOTE More on this pattern: `www.wikipatterns.com/Magnet`

Contributors to this pattern on `Wikipatterns.com`: Mike Cannon-Brookes, Doug Belshaw, David Peterson, Trevor Pike, Ben Nichols

11.   Be Firm and Think Long Term

Once your group starts using the wiki, be firm about making sure people use it and don't drift back to earlier means of collaboration. For example, if you used to send out meeting agendas by email, and now you put them on the wiki and email a link to the appropriate page, you may get someone who protests and asks for the agenda by email. They may argue that it's more work to get an email and have to link to a wiki page, instead of just having the agenda right in the email.

If this happens, I'd suggest responding that although it seems like an inconvenience in the short term, it's really only a temporary inconvenience that paves the way for several improvements. First is a reduction in email when people get used to going to the wiki — an email with a link to the meeting agenda wiki page will no longer be necessary. The second is a further reduction in email when people who need to edit the agenda do so directly on the wiki instead of emailing the person who sent the agenda.

The third improvement is that now information is stored in a more archival, accessible, and secure format than email: If you were to lose your laptop or it's stolen, email is lost along with it and this can compromise the security of sensitive information. However, if you're using a wiki, that information is stored on a secure server and won't be lost or compromised as easily.

The fourth improvement is that once you start using the wiki for meeting agendas, it lays the foundation for further wiki use, such as managing the tasks and projects that arise from the agenda. It's this organic use that makes the wiki quickly become an indispensable tool for information and collaboration.

One of the most interesting observations I've made recently regarding wikis has to do with financial services firms and how they're perceived. Most people are inclined to think of financial services firms — investment banks, securities trading firms, retail banks, and so on as very conservative, serious, and probably not the most likely to be early adopters of leading edge technology tools.

In my experience, however, the reality is quite different. That's not to say they aren't serious — after all, keeping track of someone else's money is serious business! They are, however, regularly looking for tools that make their work easier because their work is highly regulated and monitored by government agencies such as the Securities and Exchange Commission (SEC) and Congress in the U.S. As a result, financial services firms are using wikis for maintaining and updating documents containing federal policies and rules that must be followed, and keeping internal policies up to date. These kinds of documents are constantly changing as new laws take effect and rules are updated and changed, so the wiki is an ideal tool for housing this information and enabling information to be quickly changed and immediately accessible to thousands of employees who use it daily.

So the lesson here is that if companies in an industry traditionally viewed as very conservative are embracing wikis, you should too. A wiki is not only an innovative way to keep critical information constantly up to date and immediately accessible; think of the cost savings and environmental benefit as well!

What's My Role in `Wikipatterns.com`?

As Atlassian's Wiki Evangelist, one of my main projects was launching `Wikipatterns.com` and helping it grow into a worthwhile, valuable resource for all wiki users.

But what exactly is my role on the site?

In every other wiki I've set up, I've been the sole champion or one of a small group of champions, and it's much the same with `Wikipatterns.com`. The types of things I'm doing can be done by any champion who is starting a wiki within an organization or for a broader web-based community like the new (and fast growing) Wikipatterns community.

For instance, when someone wrote a comment suggesting that we add a new page, I replied back with a brief note encouraging him to create the page and showing him how. I could have just created the page myself, but encouraging someone else to do it helps that person get more deeply involved in the wiki, and feel a sense of ownership in the content he or she contributes.

In a couple of other instances, I've created pages and added just section headings as a way to guide people on what to add — this is the scaffold pattern in action. To avoid the Do-it-all anti-pattern, I've proposed changes to some pages by adding a comment to the page instead of just arbitrarily making the changes. This gives others a chance to weigh in on the change, and even make the change themselves if they feel so inclined.

What happens if someone adds a page that I don't like? Maybe I don't like where the page was located in the hierarchy. For example I might think it should be linked to a different page or moved to a new section. Or, what if someone adds a paragraph of content that I think should be moved to a different page? What is my role as the guy who started the wiki?

Well. . .it's a wiki. I could move it myself, contact the contributor and discuss it with him or her, or someone else in the community could move it. Other contributors might feel trepidation about changing someone else's content, and that's to be expected, especially when they first start using the wiki. The best thing to do is encourage people to make changes that are constructive, take into account the value of previous contributions, and improve the overall quality of information.

Launching a new wiki involves hard work, planning, contributing, and community building, and it's very rewarding to see others get enthused enough to contribute and invite even more people to join in.

So what's your role on the wiki?

References

Levy, Steven. "Good for the Soul," *Newsweek*, www.msnbc.msn.com/id/15262121/site/newsweek/, 15 October 2006 (Retrieved 22 July 2007).

"The House Rules" *Sony Ericsson Developer World Wiki*, http://developer.sonyericsson.com/wiki/display/leftnav/Welcome + to + our + Wiki + community, 26 July 2007 (Retrieved 14 August 2007).

Case Study: Red Ant

Red Ant
Sydney, NSW, Australia
`www.redant.com.au`
A Conversation with Ben Still, Managing Director
Type of organization: Web design and development firm
Number of wiki users: 140
Red Ant is a web design and development firm in Sydney Australia that designs and builds websites, games and online advertising, as well as the interactive elements such as games and menus. The firm has won awards for its work from the Australian Interactive Media Industry Association, Australian Graphic Design Association, and several London International Advertising Awards.

1. Why did you choose a wiki?

We tried a number of different approaches, and looking back they were all based on a central editing model. A wiki made sense because we wanted everyone to be able to contribute and participate. It is also closer to the way that we like to work with our customers. By allowing everyone to be able to add and reshape content, more people became involved. We moved from one person slaving away creating pages and the rest of us having to wait for them, to a situation where one person gets the ball rolling, and then other people can join in to complete the task.

Say, for instance, we've created a design and need to show it to our client. First, a designer makes a page, attaches an image, and they're done with their part. But then I might look at it and realize that it needs a bit more explanation, or a link to a wireframe diagram to give context. One of our developers might have also mocked up how a menu works, and so they stick in a link to that. Our client might email the link around, and then add some comments on the page. This kind of collaborative workflow is one of our strengths, and it is really important for us to be able to add these various types of content easily.

I've come to realize that there is no "right" way to handle this communication process, and it changes radically from project to project. I would imagine some industries might suit a more formulaic approach, but we didn't have much luck — things just change too quickly and people ended up working around it rather than with it. A wiki approach has been great, since it's so flexible and adaptable.

2.   What type of wiki are you using?

We use an enterprise wiki solution that we host on our internal servers.

3.   How are you using the wiki?

The main way that we use it is to communicate clearly to our clients. We use it throughout the entirety of the design process.

The first stage is where we can communicate ideas and establish scope of the project. This has included the unexpected benefit of being able to document meeting notes so that everybody is clear on meeting outcomes and expectations — something I'm sure everyone that has ever had any sort of meeting can attest to as a potential problem!

From there, we typically use the wiki to put designs or prototypes in a space where the client is able to see them and respond quickly and easily. This transparency in the process allows us to quickly and proactively respond to requests and changes. Another benefit of the wiki is that it can be easier to explain potential challenges or pitfalls through a wiki than by email or phone. This can be especially true for design problems, where being able to easily markup a solution, or include a screenshot can communicate an idea much more clearly than any other potential method.

Toward the end of the design process, we put the links to the staging version of the site into the wiki. While the work itself is offsite, we still find it useful to have one place to collect feedback, track progress, as well as keep any feature requests for future work.

Another of our strengths is in analysis of data: We've also had some great success in using the wiki to present feedback and stats analysis using live data. For example, we've used this to graph results of a web promotion as it's happening, which allows the client to understand when they might plan marketing around that promotion. Afterward, it helps us to be able to give an analysis of the project, which is tied to all the prior information, very helpful to anyone who may not have been involved in the nitty-gritty but wants an at-a-glance summary.

Sometimes if we've got a tight timeline on a project, we'll also use the wiki to create a visual checklist of tasks until launch. This is especially true when there is quite a few different parties involved — many hands make light work, as long as all those hands know what one another is doing! This has been a good way to coordinate effort, as well as show the client that progress is being made. Alternately, we'll pull in a list of issues from Jira, our issue tracker. We've found that people are much more likely to view and understand a list of tasks if they're pulled in as a feed to a wiki page, rather than having to log in separately to the issue tracker.

We use our wiki to build up information, but another thing we've found incredibly effective is to build filtered views of information. The main space structure can be a bit daunting, especially if it's a big one for a very active project. We make a "WIP" page, which pulls in summaries of key projects. They're ordered by date, and we tag them with appropriate status and category information. From this one summary page, clients get a great snapshot of current progress and can then dive in deeper for more detail. These pages require a little love to keep them useful (updating summaries, reorganizing tags, etc.), but these custom WIP pages have become the most used part of our wiki spaces.

4. Looking at `Wikipatterns.com`, what patterns are in use on your wiki?

In terms of maintenance, our team maintains the wiki and are the most steady users of it, which makes us the combination *Maintainer/WikiGnome/ WikiZenMaster*!

While we don't want to limit the freedom of our clients to use the wiki in imaginative ways, it's a reality that for us most clients will use it for fairly defined purposes. Generally, this falls into a couple of categories: uploading assets, providing feedback, and sometimes providing briefs or additional information.

To this effect, we've used the wiki's inbuilt templating system to set up a number of templates, or *scaffolds*, which make it easy for us to quickly set up new areas for clients. Our hierarchy is set up in terms of "Clients" and then "Projects"; this allows us to provide security so that clients are restricted to their own space, as well as provide each client with a snapshot glance at all the projects that might be taking place for them. This of course, all lends itself well to the *OneWikiSpacePerGroup* pattern.

It also provides an easy *StartingPoint* for the client: Within the template, we provide some brief instructions, as well as an *Invitation* shortly afterward. We find that it usually doesn't take them too long to get the hang of things.

We find that both an *Agenda* and an *Automatic Index* are fairly crucial to the way that we're working. Knowing that everything is in the wiki means that there is a degree of transparency between us and the client; they know what we're working on, and what stage we're at. I guess it's similar to a *LunchMenu* as well, since we will also email to notify less frequent users of changes, or if we've reached a significant point in a project that requires feedback, and in the email we will point them at the wiki, and invite them to comment or contribute.

90-9-1 probably isn't quite the right ratio for us, but there certainly is an element where we'll have "lurkers", who keep themselves abreast of all the changes in the wiki even though they never take the plunge. This isn't something that we'll complain too much about though — as long as things are getting communicated, one way or another!

5.   What changes have you seen as a result of using a wiki?

The main difference is that communication is stronger across the board: within our own team, with our partners in the U.S. (we're in Australia), and of course with external clients. While we still use the tools like email, face-to-face meetings, bringing wiki into the equation has meant expectations are clearer, feedback is quicker and more effective, and as a result, projects are better managed.

For clients, this means that they are better informed. Rather than having to ask us directly for information, they're able to do a bit of research for themselves within the wiki. This means that when it does come to communication, it's a more informed discussion on all sides.

It might be obvious, but the collaborative nature of a wiki also means that we can spend less time trying to chase various elements, such as content, assets or feedback, and that process of client contribution is intuitive, even fun! This results in happier clients, and means that we can get on with doing our job of building better websites.

Internally, using a wiki has meant that information gets to the people who need it more easily. With email, you can get the problem that the necessary information could bottleneck around one person, especially if they were busy, or if they happened to be away. This doesn't happen with a wiki — even the process of regularly reviewing and updating the information in the wiki raises the general level of awareness.

It also empowers each member of the team, giving them more transparency as well as more responsibility for what they have to do. In concrete terms, this means that our designers can get updates to clients in one step, while managers can monitor the changes and communicate more easily with clients.

Also, using a wiki has been the best way that we've found to keep those scraps of information that just don't fit anywhere else. Examples range from logins and passwords to websites like a stock photo site, documenting our processes, and even keeping a collaborative "list of contacts," which is easily accessible by everyone in-house. We've tried numerous things for these bits of information, and a wiki has been the best solution by far.

Lastly, one of the best things about a wiki is that it maintains a transparency to our clients in terms of the work that we're doing. Before we maintained a wiki, there wasn't as much communication to the client, and no way of them knowing what we're doing, short of directly contacting us. A wiki means that they're kept abreast of any developments on their project, making us look as productive as can be. In the end, our wiki helps us to work better, and it helps our work to look better, too.

Case Study: A Conversation with a WikiChampion: Jude Higdon

A Conversation with a WikiChampion: Jude Higdon
`www.mwazaji.com`

1. Why did you choose a wiki?

Grossly speaking, colleges and universities generally see themselves as having two primary missions: teaching and research. The majority of university resources, including technical resources, are dedicated in some form or other to the service of one of these two areas. The Center for Scholarly Technology (CST), my team at the major Southern California research institution where I worked from 2004–2007, was responsible for aiding faculty in the application of technology in support and enhancement of teaching and learning (although these lines were not always very well defined, as instructors are increasingly involving even their undergraduate students in their research). This case study will focus on wiki adoption in this context.

In early 2004 and into 2005 the faculty that we supported was hitting a wall in finding a viable technical solution to meet their needs for intra- and inter-class collaborations. While the University as a whole had invested in a suite of enterprise-level applications for course management (CMS), face-to-face collaborations, and other tools, these often fell short of enabling the kind of meaningful collaborative knowledge-making between and among learners that many of our instructors wanted.

We experimented with many different types of tools, including our enterprise course management system (CMS), discussion boards, and blogs, before landing on the sunny shores of the wiki. While it was not a perfect solution (would that there be such a thing), we found that it was the most appropriate tool for the wide range of articulated pedagogical needs from our faculty that we were then able to enact. We invested in an enterprise-level system and began a pilot, which would ultimately grow to include nearly 40 instructor-led projects and over 1000 students.

2.   What type of wiki are you using?

After experimentation with several wiki clients, we chose one with a robust feature set that we hoped would scale to meet our needs. Our technical team set to work integrating it with our authentication system (Shibboleth) but also maintained the ability to add guest user accounts using the wiki system's native user account system; this became critical to the success of our program. One of the primary limitations of our enterprise CMS system was that it had become *so* secure that only those who were enrolled in a specific course were able to access course resources. The task of adding other non-enrolled members of the USC community to a course in the CMS was daunting; adding non-university members to a learning community in our CMS was functionally impossible.

This may seem like a semantic/technical point, but it's worth articulating, and speaks in some ways to the heart of what makes a wiki great. Certainly, wiki content can be more or less controlled, wiki users more or less empowered to add, edit, and delete content, based on authenticated roles. But in the end, the information paradigm behind the wiki is one of inclusion, of community, and of the marketplace of ideas. Adding invested, talented individuals to our knowledge-making conversations who don't fit into traditionally, pre-defined roles from our organizations should generally be seen as a worthwhile endeavor by the wiki enthusiast. It's what wikis do, and we needed to make sure that we didn't hobble the tool with overly-strict authentication systems.

3.   How are you using the wiki?

Instructors began using the wikis in a variety of contexts and for a variety of academic purposes. For example, one instructor developed a collaborative research project among her graduate students in the Master of Public Policy program that provided insights into redeveloping urban areas ravaged by natural disasters. The research enabled by the wiki, which would ultimately win several prestigious design awards including a place of prominence as a showpiece at the Bienale in Italy, was specifically focused on helping to redesign the 9th Ward of New Orleans in the aftermath of Hurricane Katrina. In perhaps a more classic use of the wiki environment, still another instructor used her wiki as a way to create a collectively-generated knowledge base for her high enrollment course on the history of the evolution debates. Yet another instructor in the business writing department used her wiki as a space for collaborative writing assignments. Another instructor in the computer science department used the wiki as a space for managing multi-semester collaborative group projects — students even shared code among themselves and with instructors in the space. And an instructor in a service-learning organization used the wiki space to collaborate among students in community-focused externships and multiple course instructors who were helping to guide the student experience. We found that, for many articulated needs for collaborative and collective writing, the wiki was an excellent tool that met and sometimes even surpassed instructors' and students' needs.

4. Looking at `Wikipatterns.com`, what patterns are in use on your wiki?

We saw many of the wiki patterns mentioned in this book emerge through our pilot and expansion phase. I discuss these below, from the general patterns to the individual.

General Usage Patterns

The *One Wiki space per group* wiki pattern in many ways describes our overall approach. In a large university setting, we found wiki spaces to be most useful when applied at the unit level of the course. The flexibility of the environment allowed a single tool to serve many instructors' needs.

Another general wiki pattern that we saw emerge was *scaffolding*. Early in our pilot it became clear that wiki use among our students was much higher when the experience was scaffolded than when it was not. Learners tended to struggle when they were faced with an empty wiki space and provided only general goals for the wiki that had no initial structure. There is a danger in overstructure, however; some wiki projects never blossomed beyond the initial structure, which students later complained was overly rigid, apparently not knowing that they could have changed the structure (or perhaps lacking the confidence to do so).

Specific Usage Patterns

One specific wiki pattern that we saw emerge was the use of *overview pages*. In several courses, instructors used wikis to allow students to develop personal ePortfolio-style knowledge bases, which focused on their research or course project work. As students' work overlapped and content began to be shared, overview pages connecting themes emerging from student work sometimes developed.

Selective rollback became important for collaborative writing projects. As learners wrote together, inevitably something would be lost in a revision that needed to be restored. Perhaps more importantly, the simple knowledge that selective rollback was possible gave learners the confidence to edit with intellectual abandon, confident that if they "broke" anything, the damage was not irreparable.

Another wiki pattern in use in some of our classes was *BarnRaising*. Students in one of our undergraduate marketing classes spent the semester independently collecting and refining research materials for real-world clients. Then, several days before the final presentation, the entire class converged and got the wiki into final, polished form, tidying up links, moving content around, editing one another's work, and prepping for the big unveiling to the client. This course also made use of the *wiki not email* wiki pattern; the instructor and the students praised the wiki's ability to maintain a known current version of the project content; gone are the days of wondering who had the most recent version of this document or that document.

The *lunch menu* wiki pattern was popular among instructors using wikis as course websites. Foregoing more rigidly structured enterprise CMS platforms, these instructors used wiki course sites to update assignments, announcements, and other timely forms of course news.

The *ThreadMode* pattern emerged in the History of the Evolution Debates course mentioned earlier. In this course, the instructor used a structured wiki to encourage students to hold an asynchronous debate about the course material, chronicling their personal beliefs and insights on each week's readings. The resulting wiki was a robust meta-knowledge base, not of the course content, but of the class's understanding of the issues relating to the course content, with each participant having a distinct voice that was clearly traceable to the beginning of the semester.

Individual Patterns of Use

We also found some wiki patterns emerge in the roles that individuals tended to play in the course wiki. Instructors, for instance, liked to serve in the *WikiGardener* capacity, pruning dead content and ensuring that large course wikis don't go out of control. We've also seen *WikiZenMasters* emerge. The wiki site that eventually presented in the Bienale required some aesthetic overhaul before its premiere. Some of the more skillful contributors rolled up their sleeves and made the wiki beautiful.

5. What changes have you seen as a result of using a wiki?

Perhaps the biggest change that we've seen is the interest that instructors have in creating nontraditional writing and collaboration assignments. Wikis, perhaps ironically, are a technology that instructors seem to take to more organically than do students; many of our instructors were amazed at the curricular flexibility afforded by the wiki, and were excited to immerse their students in creative, nontraditional research and coursework methodologies. Students often struggled, at least initially, with the wiki environment. However, with insistence and perseverance from instructors, the benefits of the collaborative environment became increasingly clear to learners. Among all of our more than 40 wiki projects, we only had one that was terminated before the end of the semester, and that was because the instructor simply got cold feet. Anyone who has worked in higher education can attest to what an achievement this is; innovation in the classroom generally has the half-life of ^{16}N (that is, about 7 seconds). Our successes could not have been possible if the tool was not meeting a real, unaddressed need for our instructors and learners.

CHAPTER 5

Drive Large-Scale Adoption

During the pilot, it's possible — and necessary — to handpick the groups that will benefit most from early wiki use, have people that are motivated to use new tools, and make excellent, representative examples of wiki use. Large-scale adoption is a much more complex endeavor because the ultimate goal is to get everyone using the wiki. This means that instead of working with a few dozen users, you're likely dealing with a few hundred, and the profile of users changes as well. Not all will be as eager as the early adopters, but their reasons are legitimate and it's incumbent upon you to convince them.

This is where careful planning and use of wiki patterns come into play. Planning allows you to scale the guidelines and practices you've developed during the pilot, so that others can use them in a more widespread way. Because large-scale adoption involves so many more people, patterns bring a level of commonality and consistency to the many different spaces being created by groups throughout the organization.

Develop a Wiki Use Policy

Writing a wiki use policy can be a great way to organize wiki use, help you clarify answers to questions that new users will likely ask when they get started, and remind people of some common sense approaches to how they handle information on the wiki.

Let's take a look at an excellent example of a use policy. Sun Microsystems is using wikis for collaboration among people both inside and outside the company, and has spaces on a range of topics, including interning at Sun, application performance tuning, documentation, global citizenship, security, and storage systems patterns, to name just a few. Sun has a policy on wiki use (www.sun.com/aboutsun/media/wiki/policy.html) that I particularly like for several reasons. It's a length that's not daunting and an average user can be expected to fully read it. Many policy documents read like legal briefs and are so long that it's a joke to think that anyone other than the lawyers who write them would know what they say beyond the first few sentences.

The policy begins on a positive note: "Many of us at Sun are doing work that could change the world." This is a great way to speak to people: in a voice that recognizes this is a very different kind of wiki community use than something like Wikipedia. It acknowledges that people at Sun are working on shared goals, explains the role of the wiki as supporting that aim, encourages people to use the wiki, and asks them to read the rest of the policy as advice for successful use.

The policy continues with seven points of advice that read like the policy authors were thinking more about how to ensure success from the start, and then about setting rules with the expectation that someone will break them. The first point emphasizes the need for a Sun employee to moderate each space: Nurture growth, maintain organization, and serve as the point of contact for questions. This is an excellent example of a combination of the WikiChampion, WikiGardener, and PageMaintainer patterns. A WikiChampion is essential to the success of a space because she or he nurtures growth, builds community, and encourages others to take active roles in the development of context. A WikiGardener keeps the space organized so that as context grows, people can easily find what they're looking for. This is important because finding the content they need is essential to building participation in the community. People add and edit pages containing context that's relevant to them. A PageMaintainer is responsible for the activities on a specific — typically busy — page, and makes sure that people make necessary contributions to the page to keep collaboration moving along.

The section on moderating finishes with an important point. "A moderator must also remember that the wiki is owned by the community first and foremost and must resist controlling it." It's very smart to have this covered right at the start. Too much control drives people away; every person must feel a sense of personal ownership for a wiki to be successful, and this can only happen when no one person asserts dominance.

The next section addresses the difference between content on an intranet versus the Internet, and emphasizes that people should take an approach that assumes anyone could see content posted on the wiki. Even though this isn't necessarily the case, it's a sensible approach to use caution and not post content that is private and needs to stay that way.

Continuing the emphasis on information sensitivity, the third section deals with the distinction between talking to the community about Sun's products and technology, and rereading proprietary and confidential information regarding those products. What's good about this section is it raises awareness of this, reminds people to be careful with Sun's intellectual property, and also leaves room for judgment calls because it's not always a clear-cut issue. For example, discussing a proprietary hardware design may be inappropriate, but answering a developer's questions about software architecture for that hardware may be perfectly appropriate.

My own personal take here is that when in doubt, an employee would do well to ask her or his supervisor for advice on what's safe to disclose and what's not. Even if the supervisor doesn't have the answer, the legal department could be asked to further clarify. Also, it establishes a trail of due diligence should someone ever question what the employee disclosed. The bottom line here is that the more people who are aware of an information disclosure, the more likely it is that the right information will be disclosed.

The next section of Sun's policy advocates just this approach. In advising wiki users about compliance with financial disclosure laws, journal tracking statements about products, and road maps, it suggests consulting with management and setting sign-off before posting to the wiki if you're unsure about a particular judgment call. The section does a good job of pointing out why this information shouldn't be talked about too casually. Discussing financial issues, for example, can bring on legal trouble if it violates disclosure laws — especially for publicly traded companies. Sometimes people might not realize why certain information must be kept confidential and disclosed carefully; this section serves as a good reminder.

In the section "Think About Consequences," the policy points out that it's also important to think about not just *what* you say, but *how* you say it. The section advocates offering reasonable, constructive comments, especially if they're critical of something. Amateurish comments don't really offer anything that can be used to improve a product or service, and they run the risk of embarrassing others at Sun, especially if a customer sees them. The policy again advises people to use their judgment when deciding how they contribute to a wiki space.

The policy wraps up with a section on the use of disclaimers, and another section that looks at how the wiki fits in with other tools available at Sun. The disclaimers section points out that although people often post statements asserting that what they say does not necessarily reflect the official opinion of their employer, these statements don't always have a lot of legal weight. Again, the bottom line here is to use judgment first and foremost.

The last section makes one of the most important points: The wiki does not necessarily replace other tools, and should be seen as complementary. I like it so much because it echoes what I've been saying — trying to rush the wiki in and replace everything else won't work. The wiki should complement other tools so that the uses play to the strengths of each. In keeping with this idea, the policy ends with the statement, "Use your wiki's policy page to make your wiki's purpose clear."

The bottom line here is that a good wiki policy, like Sun's, should emphasize using sound judgment. A policy that lays down explicit boundaries is less effective because it only applies to specific scenarios, and takes a reactive approach. Sun's policy takes a proactive approach, plays to the intelligence of its employees, and is more effective because good judgment can be applied to any situation.

Work in Phases

When you move from pilot to large-scale adoption, it doesn't have to happen all at once. In fact, trying to do it all at once can actually cause a lot of problems because it's a quantum leap to go from a few dozen users in pilot to potentially thousands of users. It's better to think of your pilot as simply the first phase of a multiphased approach, and grow to full use in successively larger stages.

For example, let's say your organization has about a thousand people. If your pilot included five groups and a total of about fifty people, a good goal for the first phase of large-scale adoption is to add about a hundred people. Once you reach that goal and have a total of about 150 people using the wiki, add another 150–200 people in the next phase. By this time, you'll have about 300–350 people, and momentum from the existing users will help propel that number higher.

The timing of phases is important as well. Your pilot will be the longest phase in this process, largely because it's the proving ground and more work has to be done to get something of this scale started than to just grow it once it's underway. In my experience, phases in the large-scale rollout will be successively shorter because each one builds further momentum. The longer the wiki is around, the more people will know about it and be interested in using it as they see more and more people around them using it.

Overall, bringing in a wiki is about a two-year process, from the time you first start exploring it to the time when it's in full production use. The pilot phase, including initial setup, testing, and technical integration with LDAP directory and other enterprise services will take about six months. The first phase of large-scale adoption will take another four to six months, and the second phase will take another three to four months. This is a bit of a liberal estimate, and things will definitely move faster and slower at times.

Explain Why People Should Use the Wiki

Although the value of using the wiki may be apparent to you, it's not necessarily apparent to somebody encountering the wiki for the first time. In fact, some people will be skeptical of this new tool and question whether it's just another addition to their already busy lives. Anthony Rethans, a colleague of mine who works in business development says, "Just because we have more means of communication doesn't mean we have more time to consume them." This is a valid point, and to make the wiki a widespread success in your organization, you have to convince people that using it won't add complexity to their day, but will actually simplify communication, speed up projects, reduce redundancy, and keep information more secure.

One thing organizations find when they first start using a wiki is that information storage and communication between groups is often quite fractured. In the absence of a centrally supported wiki, groups will often set up tools that are intended to be quick fixes to their information and collaboration needs, but these tools often stick around longer than they were originally intended to. This creates the phenomenon of a "server under someone's desk" that isn't secure against the threats of viruses, hackers, and power and hardware failures. Furthermore, because people can't easily see what others are doing in these "islands," separate, disconnected silos of information are created. Ultimately this does the organization a disservice because people end up creating redundant information instead of just building on what already exists.

A wiki reduces this scenario of walled-off information because it starts without the heavy barriers between information and lets teams decide what needs to be secured and what information should stay open. Many organizations find that only a small fraction of information really needs to be completely restricted and walled-off from anyone but the people directly working with it, and the previously locked-up information that becomes more accessible with wiki use becomes more useful and up to date.

Another important point to make when explaining why people should use the wiki is that it keeps information more secure. It seems every time I turn around there's another story about a major corporation or government agency losing a laptop with thousands of social security numbers, credit card numbers, and other personal identifying information that's prized by identity thieves. When people collaborate using tools such as email and shared drives, they often have copies of documents and the contents of their email inbox stored locally on the laptop. If that laptop is lost or stolen, all the sensitive data on it is compromised.

When you use a wiki, the data on pages is stored on a server, and because you access wiki pages through a web browser, files don't need to be downloaded and stored locally to be edited. The server itself is also better protected from physical and data loss or theft than a laptop because it doesn't leave the data center.

Use Pilot Cases as Examples

You'll find that your pilot is the gift that keeps on giving, because in addition to getting the wiki started in your organization, helping you work out technical and integration issues, and giving you a controlled environment in which to test different wiki uses, it gives you a set of examples that can be used during large-scale adoption to help new wiki users get ideas and inspiration. One great way to make use of the pilot examples is to create a tour of some or all of the pilot groups' wiki spaces, highlighting key points such as the purpose of each, specific types of content different groups have used their spaces to collaboratively build, how groups organize their information, and the roles taken on by people in each.

LeapFrog, a company that creates technology-based educational products, has taken this approach with its own internal wiki. Sarah Cox, a member of the team that's deploying and supporting the LeapFrog wiki, developed a tour that is part of the introduction to the wiki for new users. It includes screenshots of various spaces, showcasing a variety of uses that can give new users ideas as they get started. Because the examples are from other internal LeapFrog teams, the tour helps ensure a certain amount of consistency that makes the wiki more usable so that when people from different teams collaborate, they'll be able to easily navigate other spaces. Figure 5-1 shows how the Finance Team uses their wiki space to organize information for global meetings and provide pages for all the teams within the department, and Figure 5-2 shows how the development team for the Fly Fusion product uses their wiki space to organize news, collaborate, and even keep a list of local restaurants that deliver!

Figure 5-1 LeapFrog Tour Stop 1: Finance Team Site

© LeapFrog Enterprises, Inc. Used with permission.

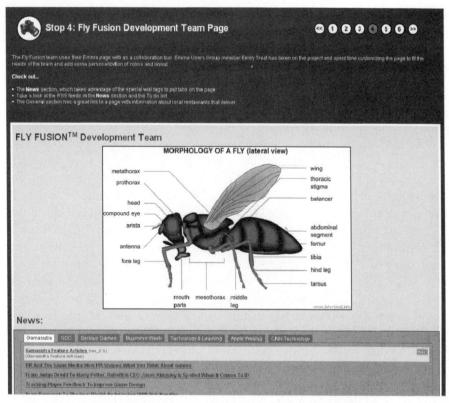

Figure 5-2 LeapFrog Tour Stop 4: Fly Fusion Development Team Page
© LeapFrog Enterprises, Inc. Used with permission.

Offer Training and Support

It's good to offer scheduled training sessions and a support system for handling questions on both technical and strategic issues. Training helps boost peoples' confidence in their ability to use the wiki, lets them know they have a place to go if they need help, and builds a peer support system between the people who attend sessions. Besides offering scheduled sessions, offer to drop in and visit groups using the wiki to see how things are going and offer advice and tips on current wiki use.

Apply Patterns

Let's take a look at a series of patterns that help people get new wiki spaces started, encourage colleagues to use the wiki, tap into the social side of the wiki by creating user profiles, seed spaces with content, and alert others to the content needed on pages. These are some of the patterns I see in action most often, and regularly recommend when working with organizations on their large-scale adoption plans.

The Importance of WikiChampions

Getting people to use the wiki is a process that reduces information redundancy, lowers the barriers to collaboration, keeps information more up to date, and makes technology feel truly usable and responsive to users' needs. The key to making this happen is helping people see that whole process, and realize the payoff if they get started using the wiki. In the large-scale adoption phases, you have something you didn't have nearly as much of during the pilot: satisfied users who are often so pleased with their experience that they'll seize any opportunity to convince their colleagues of the benefits of using the wiki. These are your WikiChampions, and when you're working to educate a lot of people about a new tool, you couldn't ask for a better or more effective tool than the word-of-mouth evangelism these people willingly provide.

These WikiChampions are very valuable to spreading the wiki because of their existing relationships with colleagues they regularly work with. Every person in every organization has a network of people they regularly work with, and they'll be able to introduce these colleagues from other groups to the wiki by using their knowledge of people and projects to pick the best places to introduce wiki use.

NOTE More on this pattern: `www.wikipatterns.com/Champion`

Contributors to this pattern on `Wikipatterns.com`: Joshua C. Lerner, Imran Aziz, James Mortimer, Marcelo Herondino Cardoso, Karsten Jahn

Invitation

One pattern WikiChampions are naturally good at is inviting people to try the wiki. Early adopters are by nature eager to try new tools, but many mainstream users — the majority of people targeted during large-scale adoption — aren't as likely to try, for a variety of reasons. Some are risk-averse and want to wait until others have proven the viability of a new tool first. Others prefer more formal training whenever they start using something new, and still others are just too busy.

An invitation creates an opportunity to dedicate time to trying the wiki and gives people reassurance that someone knowledgeable is there to help them get started.

NOTE More on this pattern: `www.wikipatterns.com/Invitation`

Contributors to this pattern on `Wikipatterns.com`: Mike Cannon-Brookes, Enric Senabre Hidalgo, Marijana Prusina, wikifirst

StartingPoint

A StartingPoint is a site that helps first-time users familiarize themselves with a wiki and get ideas for how to use it. It can include guidelines for wiki use, instructions for creating an account and setting up a wiki space, and information on training and support for wiki users. LeapFrog's tour of example wikis is a prime example of this, because it offers new users concrete examples that are highly relevant because they're from others inside the company. WikiChampions often use a StartingPoint like this because it's complementary to the Invitation in guiding the first experience, and making sure they don't say "Ok, now what?" when they visit the wiki for the first time.

NOTE More on this pattern: `www.wikipatterns.com/StartingPoint`

Contributors to this pattern on `Wikipatterns.com`: **Marijana Prusina, wikifirst, Fabio Masetti, Cheryl Chase**

Personal Spaces

In the last chapter, you looked at the importance of personal spaces as a way for people to post information about themselves and practice editing before they begin using the wiki for group collaboration. This is even more important during large-scale adoption because the value of the social aspect of the wiki increases as the number of people using it increases. Large-scale adoption, when you're aiming to get the whole organization using the wiki, is a perfect time to build out the social network as people get started on the wiki. An added benefit, especially for organizations where people are spread across great distances, is that the presence of personal spaces helps strengthen social ties.

NOTE More on this pattern: `www.wikipatterns.com/MySpace`

Contributors to this pattern on `Wikipatterns.com`: **lukehe, Sunir Shah, Trevor Pike, wikifirst, Remi Bachelet, Ronja Addams-Moring**

Welcoming

When a person makes that all-important first edit, perhaps to post information in their personal space, leave a comment welcoming them to the wiki and acknowledging something specific from their contribution. Nothing communicates the essence of the wiki to a first-time contributor better than getting a comment shortly after making their first edit. The personal welcome helps them immediately feel like part of the community, and the fact that someone acknowledged their contribution signals that they've joined an active community, which motivates them to keep making contributions.

> **NOTE** More on this pattern: `www.wikipatterns.com/Welcoming`

Contributors to this pattern on `Wikipatterns.com`: Mark Dilley, Marijana Prusina, wikifirst

BarnRaising

Once people have familiarized themselves with the wiki, jump-start a group's space with a BarnRaising. A BarnRaising is a planned event in which a group gets together in the same physical space at the same time to begin construction of their virtual space on the wiki. Whereas building a personal space helps people get comfortable with the mechanics of building a wiki and editing in a place of their own, a BarnRaising helps them get used to collaborative editing. It gets a critical mass of activity on the wiki, and allows the team to make decisions about what content to put on the wiki, and how they organize their space, name pages, and so on.

For example, if a team is planning to use the wiki to manage meeting agendas and minutes, they can decide on a naming convention for individual meeting pages. Making decisions like this can seem trivial, but when organically developing a structure that suits each group's needs is essential, as it is with the wiki, decisions like this are critical. A group doesn't want to end up in a situation where content is poorly organized and unusable because each person is using their own organization system.

When people make these decisions together, it gives them a sense of buy-in and responsibility to uphold them in practice, strengthens the sense of community surrounding the wiki, and builds a support network that helps people mutually grow their wiki use.

> **NOTE** More on this pattern: `www.wikipatterns.com/BarnRaising`

Contributors to this pattern on `Wikipatterns.com`: Trevor Pike

SingleProblem

Sometimes a group may not feel ready to commit to the wiki enough for a full BarnRaising, and want to have a successful "proving ground" experience first. In this case, find a project, task, or pain point that using the wiki will improve, and use this to demonstrate the value of the wiki. Once people solve one problem elegantly and simply using the wiki, they'll begin to see other areas where it can have a similar impact, and wiki use will steadily grow.

My friend Mark Dilley used this pattern to get union organizers to think about using wiki; here's his take:

When I discovered wiki in January 2002 I immediately recognized its potential value in organizing work and people, especially in the intentional organizations that I worked with, labor unions. However after several years of speaking to people about the grand possibilities of mass collaboration with wiki (read: banging my head against a wall), a friend suggested that we use a wiki for simply getting contracts online in the same space for this particular labor coalition that we were involved in. Not all of the people involved in the coalition have uploaded their contract to date, but enough people have done so and even used the wiki for things other than the contracts.

NOTE More on this pattern: `www.wikipatterns.com/SingleProblem`

Contributors to this pattern on `Wikipatterns.com`: **Mark Dilley**

Seed It with Content

The goal of the BarnRaising is to get people together to jump-start wiki collaboration, and in addition to making operational decisions about things like content organization, uses, and naming conventions, it's a great venue to seed the wiki with content. For the wiki to become a destination, the content people use every day has to be available on it. If everyone pitches in to move content during the BarnRaising, they'll have set the stage for continuing to work with it on the wiki. This happens because they've invested the effort to move it, and it's now easier and faster to update.

For example, if a team has a handbook of common procedures that's distributed as a text document, move the contents into the wiki. In the process, break out sections of content in the document into separate wiki pages to improve readability and avoid the phenomenon of extremely long pages. Shorter pages make content easier to find when browsing, and are more conducive to editing because it's generally easier and less distracting to work with smaller, more focused blocks of content.

It's much easier to keep existing information up to date and add new content when something like a handbook, how-to guide, or reference manual is on a wiki. When content is stored in a text document, that document can easily get lost in peoples' inboxes, making information hard to find in a pinch. It's also harder to keep up to date because changes made by each person to his or her local copy need to be reconciled across all copies. It's almost impossible for this to happen in a fluid, elegant manner that doesn't involve someone dropping what he or she normally does to manually combine changes.

Using a wiki reverses the traditional course where information is of highest value when first published and declines in value over time. When a wiki is seeded with content, the value of that content actually *grows* over time as new information is added, errors are fixed, and information is essentially insured against falling out of date.

NOTE More on this pattern: `www.wikipatterns.com/SeedItWithContent`

Contributors to this pattern on `Wikipatterns.com`: **Chris Almond, Imran Aziz, Karl Auer, Benjamin Doherty, Trevor Pike, Ben Nichols, Karen Lai**

Intentional Error

Intentional error is one of the original wiki adoption patterns pioneered by Ward Cunningham, creator of the first wiki. It involves intentionally making errors that are left for others to find and fix, thus getting them used to editing a wiki.

When you're editing a wiki page, just make some errors such as misspelling a word or forgetting to capitalize at the beginning of a sentence. Then invite others to proofread your page and when they discover the errors, let them fix the errors themselves just by editing the wiki. However, be mindful that not all readers may recognize an error or choose to fix it, so introducing substantial or factual errors in content may prove to do more damage than good.

NOTE More on this pattern: `www.wikipatterns.com/IntentionalError`

Contributors to this pattern on `Wikipatterns.com`: **Mike Cannon-Brookes, James Mortimer, Larry Dukerich**

ContentAlert

The ContentAlert pattern involves leaving specific messages that let people know a page needs content to be added, refined, or fixed. One of the best ways of doing this is to put a message in a box at the top of the page in question (Figure 5-3).

NOTE More on this pattern: `www.wikipatterns.com/ContentAlert`

Contributors to this pattern on `Wikipatterns.com`: **Shurito, Trevor Pike, Mark Truman**

New Employee Wiki

An important part of large-scale adoption is making sure that new employees are introduced to the wiki. Because new employees are coming in with a fresh perspective and haven't used any tools within your organization yet, they'll be able to start fresh with the wiki, and it can provide a good way to organize their first few days. For example, create a space specifically for new employees that contains orientation materials, a checklist of things to do, forms to fill out, and so on. An added benefit of doing this: The space can be easily updated whenever any of these procedures or documents change. Also link to pages that document work procedures so new employees can get up to speed faster.

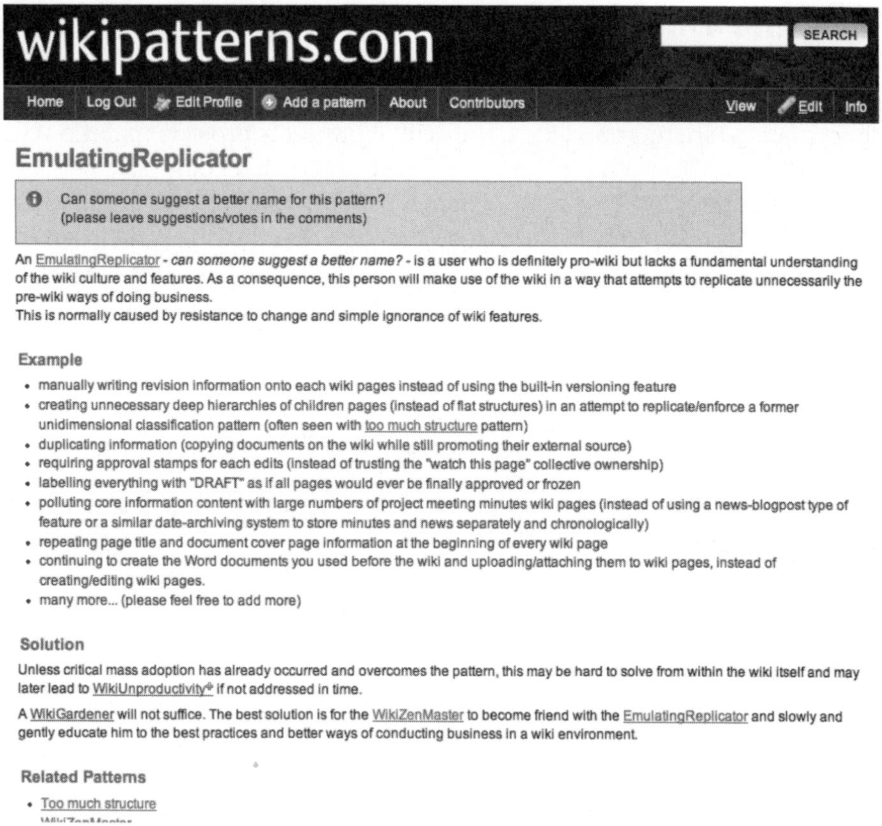
wikipatterns.com

SEARCH

Home | Log Out | Edit Profile | Add a pattern | About | Contributors | View | Edit | Info

EmulatingReplicator

Can someone suggest a better name for this pattern?
(please leave suggestions/votes in the comments)

An EmulatingReplicator - *can someone suggest a better name?* - is a user who is definitely pro-wiki but lacks a fundamental understanding of the wiki culture and features. As a consequence, this person will make use of the wiki in a way that attempts to replicate unnecessarily the pre-wiki ways of doing business.
This is normally caused by resistance to change and simple ignorance of wiki features.

Example

- manually writing revision information onto each wiki pages instead of using the built-in versioning feature
- creating unnecessary deep hierarchies of children pages (instead of flat structures) in an attempt to replicate/enforce a former unidimensional classification pattern (often seen with too much structure pattern)
- duplicating information (copying documents on the wiki while still promoting their external source)
- requiring approval stamps for each edits (instead of trusting the "watch this page" collective ownership)
- labelling everything with "DRAFT" as if all pages would ever be finally approved or frozen
- polluting core information content with large numbers of project meeting minutes wiki pages (instead of using a news-blogpost type of feature or a similar date-archiving system to store minutes and news separately and chronologically)
- repeating page title and document cover page information at the beginning of every wiki page
- continuing to create the Word documents you used before the wiki and uploading/attaching them to wiki pages, instead of creating/editing wiki pages.
- many more... (please feel free to add more)

Solution

Unless critical mass adoption has already occurred and overcomes the pattern, this may be hard to solve from within the wiki itself and may later lead to WikiUnproductivity if not addressed in time.

A WikiGardener will not suffice. The best solution is for the WikiZenMaster to become friend with the EmulatingReplicator and slowly and gently educate him to the best practices and better ways of conducting business in a wiki environment.

Related Patterns

- Too much structure

Figure 5-3 A ContentAlert at the top of a page on `Wikipatterns.com`

NOTE **More on this pattern: `www.wikipatterns.com/NewStarter`**

Contributors to this pattern on `Wikipatterns.com`: James Matheson, Kim Barchard, James Mortimer

Document Business Processes

Another great use for the wiki is to document common business processes. This strengthens the wiki's role as a magnet, and gives people one more reason to use it. People can easily document processes and procedures that would otherwise reside only in their heads, and the wiki becomes a great place to preserve and update this information as processes change and people come and go. Also, it becomes an invaluable resource for new employees to quickly get up to speed on common processes, and they can refer to the wiki as often as they need.

"It's on the wiki"

As your organization's wiki becomes the central tool people rely on to find information, share knowledge, and collaborate on projects, people will be saying, "It's on the wiki" more and more often. If people ask you for information, point them to the wiki. If they haven't heard of it yet, give them a quick overview and show them how they can get started using it themselves. Pretty soon, when you ask them for information, they'll say, "It's on the wiki."

Case Study: JavaPolis

JavaPolis Conference and Community
  Antwerp, Belgium
  `www.javapolis.com`
  A Conversation with Stephan Janssen, Founder and active member
  Type of organization: Technology conference
  Number of wiki users: 20.000 +
  JavaPolis is an annual conference organized by the Belgium Java User Group
(BeJUG). It takes place in a large cinema complex in Antwerp, Belgium during
the second week of December. For five days, about 100 speakers talk about
Java APIs, frameworks, products, and so on. It's also a great event to network
and socialize with other Java developers. Last year the fifth edition of JavaPolis
had about 2,800 people attending from 50 countries, and the conference is
growing with 30–50 percent more attendees every year. JavaPolis is officially
the second biggest Java conference in the world after JavaOne.

1.   Why did you choose a wiki?

The Belgian Java User Group (BeJUG) has a large community, and by using
a wiki we can engage our members, partners, and steering members with the
content/feedback of our annual conference. Companies can update their own
partner page, speakers can add or edit their bio or abstract, and the program
committee can add talks or update the schedule.

2.   What type of wiki are you using?

We use a self-hosted Java wiki using a Resin web server and MySQL database.

3. How are you using the wiki?

The wiki itself serves as the conference website and contains the schedule of events, information on speakers, partners, sponsors, and news.

4. Looking at `Wikipatterns.com`, what patterns are in use on your wiki?

- **Conferences.**   JavaPolis is a conference, so we use the wiki to publish our schedule, speakers, and related info.
- **OverviewPages.**   Based on parent-child relationships, an overview page is assembled where different talks can be viewed per event (University, Conference, BOF, and Quickies). Also different related pages are labeled so we can create overview pages based on selected labels.
- **Community Write.**   The schedule of the different events can only be edited by the program committee group. This is based on the permission schema supported within the wiki.
- **Viral.**   Conference speakers can update their own talk and bio, and attendees can vote or comment wiki pages, increasing the number of wiki users by the week (even after the conference).

5. What changes have you seen as a result of using a wiki?

During a JavaPolis partner-sponsors meeting, we announced that we were going to use a wiki for the website. A lot of the companies were very skeptical about it. "Can't anyone just change it? Will that work?" they asked. I had to convince them that there is social control in a wiki because of all the people who use it and the many who receive notifications and so on.

Of course we can't guarantee there won't be a crazy guy who wants to do something aberrant, but with wikis you can always roll back to the previous version or the community can just remove it or adjust it, and I must say that works really well.

Since switching to the wiki, we're seeing more collaboration from the Community in a form of voting, comments, and content updates. Anyone who is registered can do whatever change they want to on the JavaPolis site. If someone makes an unwanted change, hundreds of other users are notified and can fix the problem. From a wiki perspective the social control actually results in ideal content control.

Case Study: A Conversation with a WikiChampion: Jeff Calado

A Conversation with Jeff Calado, Release Engineering Manager
Type of organization: Division of a Fortune 500 Technology company
Number of wiki users: 150

1. Why did you choose a wiki?

When I started here two years ago all project communication and collaboration was done through email, meetings, and networked drives. It was widely accepted that certain people were the keepers of information on topics they were experts on. The only way to get this knowledge was to email or talk to them, and they'd often send you a document they had sitting on their computer or forward you an old email.

From past experience I knew firsthand the collaboration benefits a good wiki could have given the team's commitment. I put together a sample wiki demonstrating how team and project collaboration could happen, and then I ran a series of one-on-one demos with the more influential members of the organization to sell them on the solution. Upon going through the demo and answering their questions, the benefits were so clear that it took no further convincing.

2. What type of wiki are you using?

We self-host a commercial enterprise wiki that was chosen, among other reasons, because it allows us to flexibly control access rights to various areas in the site.

3.   How are you using the wiki?

We create a space for each team within the organization and for each project, plus one space for information relevant to the entire organization.

Each project homepage provides an introduction to the project and posts the latest status information. Meeting notes and specs are also posted. Technical details about the project, testing tips, and the like are all captured.

People still love their email around here, so we often create an email account for the wiki and add it to the project email group. The wiki is able to download those emails to the project space so they are archived with the rest of the project information. This is great because it lets someone that jumps on the project midway to view all of the email history that happened for the project before they started.

Each team also maintains its own space with information relevant to the group — in particular, information on getting their systems up and running, which is priceless when new employees join the team. Each round of new hires feels indebted to those that posted the information that got them started, and they do a great job improving the content and making it even easier for the next round.

4.   Looking at `Wikipatterns.com`, what patterns are in use on your wiki?

I serve the role of *Champion, Maintainer,* and *WikiGnome.*

As described above, we're using the *One Wiki Space per Group* pattern to organize the site. Some projects are more private than others and this structure gives us an easy way to limit access to projects as necessary.

Every new employee is immediately added to the wiki and sent a welcome email with login information and a link to a wiki page containing a screencast that I recorded to provide an introduction to using the wiki. This is our approach to the *Invitation* pattern.

The *IdentityMatters* pattern comes into play because people that used to keep everything in their head know they'll still be recognized for the information now that it's out in the open and won't lose their expert status.

The Design group loves to serve the role of *WikiZenMaster/WikiFairy* and beautify the site.

The wiki provides the *Automatic Index* pattern for us, displaying the recently updated pages on the homepage. Also, many people subscribe to daily email updates to see what has changed over the past 24 hours.

The *Trellis* pattern is fitting for the evolution of the startup guides the teams have built. When new employees are getting up to speed, they document what they discover and sprinkle comments throughout the document asking for validation and elaboration on the points they are most unsure of. This gets the easy stuff out and the more experienced employees come in and fill out the details since the tedious work of getting all the little details out there was already done.

Finally, two great examples of the *SingleProblem* pattern are out of the office calendars and release notes. People here use iCal to track their schedules. We have an internal WebDAV server where they can publish their iCals and each team member maintains an out of the office calendar that they publish to the site. The wiki has a plug-in that displays a calendar in the wiki and lets us subscribe it to any number of iCals. For each team they create an out of the office calendar page in their team or project space and subscribe to the relevant team member's iCals. This lets individuals manage their time-off and automatically communicate it to the broader groups they work with.

The other *SingleProblem* pattern example is our management of release notes. Each build has release notes documented for it. We capture those in the version control system when tagging the build but that doesn't provide a very visible means for documenting the release. Part of the build process is to automatically publish release notes to the wiki. This puts the history of all builds in one easy-to-read location. There is the added benefit of providing a pull system for people that want to get email each time a build is released. They simply subscribe to receive email updates each time the release notes index page is updated, and now they get emailed each time a build goes out. Before this solution, the entire team got emailed the build release notes whether they wanted them or not and there was no central repository of this information outside of the version control system.

5.   What changes have you seen as a result of using a wiki?

The greatest improvement has been centralization of project information on the wiki; it really helps the team to collaborate better.

There is now an expectation that people take relevant information out of their head and share it on the wiki. The most valuable benefit from this has been the decrease in time and effort needed to get new employees up to speed as well as an improvement in the consistency of the process. The benefit of improving the knowledge and skills of the broader team is another valuable result.

Prevent (or Minimize) Obstacles

Whereas wiki patterns are the approaches and strategies you want to apply, anti-patterns are the things you don't want to happen, or at least want to catch and fix as early as possible. To do this effectively, you must recognize them, and that's the goal of the anti-patterns on Wikipatterns.com.

What Can Hinder Wiki Adoption?

Let's look at some of the most common anti-patterns, the reasons they happen, and how to quickly fix them.

The key thing to remember about anti-patterns as they relate to wiki use in an organization is that they're mostly the result of ignorance about how to use the wiki, and not malicious intent. Often people who are engaging in anti-pattern behavior just need some help understanding how to contribute to the wiki in more productive ways.

Do-it-all

Sometimes a person can get too enthusiastic about the wiki, and try to do everything. Remember that kid in school who always raised his or her hand to answer every question? It's somewhat the same situation with a person who acts as a Do-it-all on the wiki.

A Do-it-all is someone who:

- always is the first to volunteer to do something on the wiki to the point that they don't even give others the opportunity to volunteer
- regularly offers to do things on the wiki for others, instead of helping them do it themselves

Bear in mind that a Do-it-all isn't a *bad* person, but the danger in having a Do-it-all is that one person dominating the wiki blocks others from having the opportunity to directly use it themselves. If someone is reluctant to use the wiki, and a Do-it-all just offers to do it for them, that person will never get over their reluctance to use the wiki, and will rely on the Do-it-all instead of taking the time to properly learn how to use the wiki. This can ultimately doom the wiki because it doesn't have enough people using it to make collaboration effective. Also, the people who are reluctant to use the wiki are often skeptical about whether it should even be used at all, and if they don't see its value by directly interacting with it, they're likely to not support it in the long run.

One way to channel a person's enthusiasm away from Do-it-all behavior is to have that person help others get comfortable with the wiki. Instead of making changes by themselves, ask that person to meet with others who are less familiar with the wiki, and work with them to both get comfortable with the mechanics of editing and collaboration, and introduce changes that will stimulate further contributions.

NOTE More on this pattern: `www.wikipatterns.com/DoItAll`

Contributors to this pattern on `Wikipatterns.com`: Jonathan Nolen, Mark Dilley, Alexa Thomas, James Mortimer, Lindsey Sales

OverOrganizer

OverOrganizer and Do-it-all have some similarities, and sometimes the same type of person can exhibit both behaviors. The main difference between the two is that unlike a Do-it-all who does everything, an OverOrganizer tends to take what others have contributed to the wiki and rearrange it to try to structure content in a way that makes sense to them. Often this involves moving pages, renaming them, and rearranging content — sometimes within the same page, and sometimes to different pages.

As with Do-it-all, an OverOrganizer isn't doing this out of any negative intent, and is actually trying to improve the wiki. But the problem with this is it leaves others confused, unable to find content they added, and it deters them from participating because they lose a sense of ownership over their contributions. As much as a wiki is supposed to be collaborative and enable editing of all content, people need to at least find the content they've contributed and feel confident that there's some logic to how content is changed on the wiki. If one person unilaterally changes the structure too much, and moves or rearranges pages others have just created, people will lose interest in the wiki because they feel they don't have much to contribute or can't do it in a way that satisfies them.

A wiki should start out with the least amount of structure necessary and structure should be added over time, when needed, and in a manner that involves and informs everyone who uses it. If you encounter an OverOrganizer, keep in mind that they might not even realize that what they're doing can be harmful. Encourage them to leave a comment on a page proposing a significant content change before actually making that change. This offers an opportunity for discussion and refining the direction of major changes, but it can also simply inform people so they know where to find content after the change. Also, it's a good idea during a group's wiki Barn-Raising to emphasize that people should distinguish between smaller, routine edits and larger, more significant changes, and in the event of a larger change, discuss it with the community first.

NOTE More on this pattern: `www.wikipatterns.com/OverOrganizer`

Contributors to this pattern on `Wikipatterns.com`: **Stewart Mader**

WikiTroll

WikiTroll is another anti-pattern that often arises out of ignorance about how to interact on the wiki. It's different from constructive criticism because when a person exhibits WikiTroll behavior, they make philosophically negative comments about a topic that can provoke equally negative responses, in some cases. The latter doesn't always happen, but at the very least the comments distract people from productive collaboration.

An example of a comment from troll might be, "This whole company stinks and makes a crappy product. You should go check out my company instead." On the other hand, a constructive critic might say, "The export to PDF feature in this software crashes if the file is more than 10 pages long" or "The glue supplied with the build-it-yourself table is weak and doesn't bond."

So how should you handle trolling? First, bear in mind that trolling is less frequent inside organizations, where the wiki community parallels an established one and people are working toward shared goals. So keep an eye out for trolling in wikis that are open to the public, such as a support or community website for a project or product. One way to deter casual trolling on a publicly accessible wiki is to require registration. This is effective because registering requires some effort that people often aren't going to expend if they just want to post a negative comment but don't want to otherwise engage in the community. Also, registration attaches some level of identity to the comments that people are not likely to want to establish if they're just casually trashing a product, project, or community.

If trolling happens inside your organization, it may simply be because the person posting negative comments doesn't realize that what's posted online can come across more negative than in person. In that case, having a simple chat with the person and explaining to them that it's better to tone down comments and build criticism around facts and specific issues will make comments less flaming and more useful.

NOTE More on this pattern: `www.wikipatterns.com/WikiTroll`

Contributors to this pattern on `Wikipatterns.com`: Imran Aziz, Alexa Thomas, Ronja Addams-Moring

Wikiphobia

Wikiphobia arises out of some level of fear or dislike of the wiki. Mostly this is the result of misunderstanding or lack of experience with the wiki, but it's different from the preceding anti-patterns because it often results in a lower frequency of participation on the wiki. In some cases people with Wikiphobia can even try to sabotage the wiki by suggesting that existing tools should continue to be used instead. This is a problem because the wiki thrives on active participation and if too many people have a phobia about things such as editing content written by another person, then it won't achieve critical mass of activity and will wither.

One way to handle Wikiphobia is to just circumvent it. Create a wiki and don't tell the Wikiphobic people about it until it reaches critical mass with others and the momentum can't be stopped. This also gives you a tangible example to show how wiki collaboration works in your organization, and how it's beneficial. This can go a long way to inform a Wikiphobic person and demonstrate the kind of value that convinces them to embrace it.

There is some risk here because if the Wikiphobic people are still resistive and happen to be in positions of power, they might still try to stop the wiki altogether, and then you run the risk of losing all the collaborative fabric that's been built on the wiki. But the reality is that once the wiki has gained traction and the people using it see it as essential to their work, they'll advocate for it to stay and a Wikiphobic person — even someone in a powerful position — won't be able to get rid of it easily. Even if that did happen, the grassroots nature of wiki means that a new one would likely spring up in its place. The risk here is that the new wiki could be outside the firewall, potentially putting information at risk. The bottom line is, once a wiki is in place and has gained both a critical mass of activity and momentum, Wikiphobic people will have to use it or risk being left behind, and most will, with some coaching and good examples, come around.

NOTE More on this pattern: `www.wikipatterns.com/Wikiphobia`

Contributors to this pattern on `Wikipatterns.com`: Emmanuel Proulx, John Gaynard, Sara Key

Sandbox

Creating a Sandbox, or test space where people can create pages and practice editing seems like a good idea, but it's not always as useful as it seems. For people new to the wiki, having to start in a Sandbox can create the false impression or reinforce misconceptions that the wiki is difficult to use and requires training away from the "real" content. If a person is uncomfortable with the idea of editing content written by someone else, a Sandbox won't fix this because people don't create content together and collaboratively edit it as they would in a space dedicated to a project or team.

Also, creating a Sandbox is not a remedy for Wikiphobia because it doesn't show the wiki in true form. The Sandbox is much like the warm-ups before a figure skating competition, where all the athletes are on the ice at once, but each is practicing his or her own routine independently.

It's better to have new users start by creating a personal space, because it gives them a chance to practice creating and editing content with a purpose. When people edit in the Sandbox, there isn't a larger purpose for the editing so they aren't experiencing real wiki editing or collaboration. With a personal space, they may not experience as much collaboration, but building something with common elements and purpose enables them to get comfortable with the mechanics of editing, and produce something they're proud of. Others can comment in personal spaces to welcome each user, and that provides an introduction to editing in a shared space.

NOTE More on this pattern: www.wikipatterns.com/Sandbox

Contributors to this pattern on Wikipatterns.com : **Jonathan Nolen, Imran Aziz, Ben Nichols**

BeanCounter

In some organizations, there's a push to charge departments or teams for technology services like disk storage space, or use of enterprise tools like the wiki. The thinking behind this is that it's easier for a central IT operation to support new services if the users that want them are willing to share in the cost. This idea has emerged as a response to the high price of most enterprise knowledge management tools, which IT departments have trouble affording on their own.

It can be a good idea, but there's a place where it goes very wrong, and works against the needs of users: when the IT operation decides to measure use of the tool and charge users based on their level of use. This essentially penalizes the groups that use it most, and encourages people to limit their use of it to save costs. That, in turn, limits the network effect in which the wiki's value is based on a cycle of increasing membership and activity.

How can this be avoided? Don't charge based on level of usage. In fact, with the low cost of wikis compared to other enterprise software, this shouldn't even be an option. However, watch closely to make sure that if people suggest this based on their prior experience with more expensive tools, you can explain why it's not financially necessary because of the low cost of the wiki.

> **NOTE** More on this pattern: `www.wikipatterns.com/BeanCounter`

Contributors to this pattern on `Wikipatterns.com` **: Brian M. Thomas, Harry Wood**

Empty Pages

No one wants to be first to do something, right? If people see an empty page, they won't know where to start and will likely not edit it because they don't want to post the wrong information. When people see an empty page, they often wait for the person who created it to post information first, because they assume the page creator knows best what she or he wants to do with the page. It can be good for the creator to establish the purpose of the page and seed it with content, but the problem occurs when the page sits idle for too long and others just don't know what to do with it. When a wiki has too many empty pages, it can affect the overall level of collaboration because people visiting the wiki will see those pages and might assume that it's just not the place to be and stop visiting it regularly.

So what should you do?

When you create a new page, post a basic structure, a more detailed scaffold, or just a few lines of info on the page's purpose and what content should be added to it. Even if that content is to be generated over time and not immediately available, having some information on the page helps guide people so that when they do have some content that belongs on the page, they know where to post it.

If you see an empty page, mention it to the person who created it to see if she or he realizes it's empty. You could also post a comment on the page asking for people's thoughts on what content should be added, or you could edit the page itself and post a scaffold, or rough outline of content. Then email the URL to others on your team and invite them to edit the structure and contribute content.

> **NOTE** More on this pattern: `www.wikipatterns.com/EmptyPages`

Contributors to this pattern on `Wikipatterns.com` **: Jason Yip, Trevor Pike**

All-wiki-all-the-time

It's exciting to start a wiki, especially if you're the WikiChampion and are personally invested in making it a success. But you don't want to be so enthusiastic that people get turned off to using it. This is a fine line — no question — because the job of a WikiChampion is to get people excited and suggest using the wiki so that it gets a critical mass of activity, becomes a magnet for finding and building information, and anchors itself firmly in at the core of peoples' work.

If you're too pushy about it, and try to make people drop other tools in favor of the wiki too quickly, they may feel pressured, uncomfortable, and unwilling to make the move. It's human nature to resist change to some extent and, let's face it, people who aren't early adopters get tired of trying all kinds of new tools — especially if they've been burned in the past.

So, take a measured approach. Be enthusiastic, but resist the temptation to push everything onto the wiki as fast as possible. If people want to move some projects on the wiki, but feel that others should wait until they're comfortable with getting the first round of projects on the wiki and working out the kinks, be supportive of this. The key to avoiding the All-wiki-all-the-time syndrome is to manage the change effectively. Pace things so that there's a balance between growing wiki use at a healthy rate and making sure people are comfortable with the process.

NOTE More on this pattern: `www.wikipatterns.com/AllWikiAllTheTime`

Contributors to this pattern on `Wikipatterns.com`: **Jonathan Nolen, Saul Lopez, wikifirst**

Manager Lockdown

Manager Lockdown is a scenario that takes place when a manager decides to take active ownership of content on the wiki and assume an increasingly direct role in editing that content. It happens most frequently after the wiki has become established inside an organization, when people are beginning to use it for projects involving external content development.

Sometimes it's the result of a fiefdom mentality at play. Ironically, the people who are most likely to come along and try to take ownership as a result of that perceived need to guard their territory are the same people who were doubtful of the wiki's value early on, and likely to have tried to discourage its use altogether.

In either case, when this happens it blurs the role of the wiki because certain content is now subject to the hierarchical, top-down control usually associated with more traditional content management tools. Even though other content is left to the peer management of the wiki, people become reluctant to contribute because they don't want to edit the wrong page and upset someone above them.

Also, when people just take over content on the wiki but don't understand how to effectively use it, they spend most of their energy on the homepage, instead of on the subpages where collaboration really takes place. This is a direct result of the fact that more emphasis is placed on the homepage in traditional websites and hierarchically organized sets of knowledge, and the downside here is that the manager may miss good content altogether. The bottom line is this is a surefire way to risk slowing the momentum of a wiki.

So what should you do?

This is a complex pattern because it encompasses two scenarios: one where the intentions are good, and another where the motivation isn't, but both can be counterproductive to collaboration. In the former scenario, the best course of action is to make sure pages are available to freely draft content in the early stages, and establish a practice of moving content from a drafting page to a managed page once it's ready to be reviewed and approved for public distribution. Also, it's important to educate a well-intentioned manager about the need to be transparent when managing pages, and to encourage contribution and collaboration so people don't feel reluctant to edit. Most well-intentioned managers will appreciate this help, because they don't want to disrupt something successful.

In the latter case, educating the manager is necessary to help them better understand the conditions necessary for the wiki to function successfully. Breaking the wiki down into regions of control will ultimately doom it because this runs counter to the social simplicity that makes using it so inviting. The wiki has to be the domain of the users for them to use it, and hierarchical control just gets in the way. Most managers don't want to undermine something that works, but they need to be informed so they understand how to recognize that it's working well.

NOTE More on this pattern: `www.wikipatterns.com/ManagerLockdown`

Contributors to this pattern on `Wikipatterns.com`: Brendan Patterson, Robert Castaneda, Karl Auer, Ben Nichols

Too Much Structure

This anti-pattern is the result of a long legacy of highly structured tools that force you to learn their structure before you can start using them. The inclination is to try to anticipate the structure for a new wiki and build it before content is added and collaboration takes off. If the structure is built too early, it won't necessarily match how people really organize information, and it may make people think the wiki is too rigid to meet their needs.

It can also leave the wiki in a messy, disorganized state, with lots of empty pages that are part of the anticipated structure, and lots of added pages that would otherwise appear organized but don't because they don't match the structure and are mixed in with empty pages. This can make information hard to find and deter participation on the wiki if people see it as a disorganized mess.

The solution: Have a BarnRaising so that everyone who's going to use a particular wiki can post content and build the basic structure together. Every wiki has a certain amount of structure, but it needs to evolve over time to meet the specific needs of the people using the wiki, and stay compact and simple.

When you first start adding content to a wiki space, keep it simple. Use the homepage as a simple table of contents, with a list of all pages in the space. This way, any information on the wiki is one click from the homepage. As the content grows, some areas will grow faster than others. When a topic grows large enough that pages relating to it take up a lot of space on the homepage, propose creating a second level table of contents page specifically for that content. This way, content grows in one place until it's necessary to increase structure, but every increase is compact and directly tied to content growth.

If you encounter a wiki with too much anticipated structure, and lots of empty pages as a result, propose deleting those pages. This both lets others know what's happening and engages them in improving the organization of the space.

> **NOTE** More on this pattern: `www.wikipatterns.com/TooMuchStructure`
>
> **Contributors to this pattern on** `Wikipatterns.com`: **Thomas Anger**

WikiPaintBrush

Including the word *wiki* in the name of every space on your wiki is a dangerous habit because it confuses the technology with the purpose for using it. This is problematic because people should use the wiki with a purpose, not just because it's a wiki. The wiki is just like any other technology tool in that it needs to be used with a definite purpose to really be successful.

Furthermore, putting *wiki* in every name is the wrong type of branding. Organization, product, and project names should figure prominently in the name of a wiki space, along with a term that describes the function of each space. For example, when you name the wiki containing frequently asked questions about a product, call it ProductFAQ instead of wikiFAQ.

One of the other problems with overusing the term *wiki* in the names of wikis is that if a particular wiki isn't successful, people may mistakenly associate the failure with the wiki, even if the failure has nothing do to with the fact that wiki technology was used. That mistaken association can make people less likely to use a wiki in the future.

Lastly, naming the spaces with product or project names instead of using the term *wiki* is better because it encourages the people who are passionate about that product or project to get involved with the wiki not because it's a wiki, but because of their passion for the product or project. That's much more likely to ensure lasting success.

NOTE More on this pattern: `www.wikipatterns.com/wikiPaintBrush`

Contributors to this pattern on `Wikipatterns.com`**: James Mortimer**

The Common Theme...

The common theme throughout all these patterns is not negative intent — it's ignorance or misunderstanding. That's much easier to deal with than purely negative intent, and demonstrates the importance of making sure people understand the wiki as a tool and grasp how it's intended to work. Equipped with that knowledge, they're much more likely to avoid anti-patterns themselves, and help others stay on track.

Case Study: Kerrydale Street

Kerrydale Street — Celtic Football Club
www.kerrydalestreet.com
Type of organization: Fan Club for a Scottish Football Club
Number of wiki users: 500 + registered users
Kerrydale Street is a user-generated fan wiki created to celebrate Celtic FC, a Scottish Premiere League football team. Celtic FC has a large, passionate, and international fan base that has been rabidly following the team since its first match in 1888. During those 119 years of football history, Celtric FC has amassed a treasure trove of information that needs to be chronicled and celebrated. Kerrydale Street has become that place online. In a little over one year's time, Celtic fans have contributed over 3,500 pages of content, 7,000 images added, and over 18,000 contributions. And those numbers continue to grow every day.

1. Why did the site creator choose a wiki?

The idea for the Kerrydale Street wiki came from a desire to have a companion site for a very successful Celtic forum site. The site creator toyed with the idea of going down the usual "Fan Site" road with match reports, players of the month, and so on, but decided that the best way to differentiate from these other sites was to let as many passionate fans of Celtic FC as possible help build the ultimate fan site. A wiki proved to be the easiest way to activate the Celtic faithful.

2.   What type of wiki is Kerrydale Street using?

Kerrydale Street is powered by a free consumer-oriented hosted wiki service.

3.   How is Kerrydale Street using the wiki?

The aim of Kerrydale Street is to complete a comprehensive guide to Celtic FC. To do that, Kerrydale Street houses such information as club history, stadium information, player and manager biographies, a photograph library, and a year-by-year history of the club.

4.   Looking at `Wikipatterns.com`, what patterns are in use on the wiki?

- **Champion:**   The initial Champions of Kerrydale Street came from the forum and developed the initial site positioning and content structure. Quickly thereafter, the Champions built awareness of the site, invited other passionate participants, and managed the orderly growth of the wiki website.

- **Community Write:**   Kerrydale Street requires contributors to register for the site prior to contributing. This has elevated the quality of the content added to the site. This requirement wasn't always so; the site used to open to anonymous editing. However, as rivalries in football are fierce, anonymous contributions from opposing fans hampered the positive momentum of the wiki website.

- **Use WYSIWYG:**   Fans of Celtic FC are united in their passion for their club; however, their technical skill varies greatly. WYSIWYG allows for the greatest amount of participation from the Celtic community, not just those who are passionate and also understand traditional wiki markup syntax.

5.   What changes have you seen as a result of using a wiki?

The biggest change has been the absolute reach of the Kerrydale Street wiki website. Because anyone who is passionate about Celtic FC can participate in the site, it has grown quickly. And that growth has created a virtuous cycle of greater exposure and greater participation. As an example, Kerrydale Street is now on Page 1 of Google for the keyword term "Celtic FC." And as more people are exposed to Kerrydale Street and realize that they can add to it, the goal of becoming the web's comprehensive guide to Celtic FC on the web isn't far off.

Inspirational Bull****

This is the point where most business books leave you with some boilerplate inspirational words about how whatever you've just read will radically reshape business, transform economies, and change the world.

I'm not going to do that, because the wiki isn't going to change the world by itself. It needs you, and the people you work with, talk with, meet with, email, call, and IM to try it, be open to the changes it brings, and make it a hub for information and collaboration. A wiki thrives on active participation by as many people as possible, and in turn brings greater value to each individual user. It relies on transparency, trust, and willingness to share information more openly, work more collaboratively, and see information as more valuable when more people have access to it.

Transparency leads to better and more refined business practices, because people can work together to improve things in an iterative manner, instead of fixing things only when they're broken. Access to each other's information builds trust, strengthens people's relationships, and creates stronger connections between their work. Combined, these make an organization less likely to suffer bureaucracy and an inability to get things done.

Renegades Rule

Renegades are the ones who will bring in the wiki, firmly anchor it by making it central to their work, and get all their friends to use it, too. Renegades see the potential in something like the wiki and are willing to disrupt their own status quo to try it. They aren't afraid of failure and see stagnation and status quo as failure in itself.

A WikiChampion is a renegade because often bringing in the wiki is not part of his or her "day job," and is a labor of love. He or she will set up the wiki, start using it for his or her own work, then use that initial work as an example to get other people excited about using it, and help them get started.

The WikiChampion is absolutely essential to the success of a wiki, especially in its initial stages, because that person generates enough buzz and interest to build a community of passionate users that will continue spreading the word on a larger scale.

Technology Is Simply a Tool

For far too long, software has been rather stupid to the idea that people are the most important ingredient in building anything, and technology is simply a tool. Many knowledge management initiatives have failed because people don't buy into them and make them an indispensable part of their daily work. The technology is just too complex, and requires an incredible amount of customization to do even a fraction of what people really want it to do. As a result, responsibility for anything involving these tools often ends up with the most tech-savvy person in a team.

People and context matter much more than the technology itself, and the wiki exemplifies this by minimizing complexity and structure so that everyone has the ability — and responsibility — to build, maintain, and use information. With a wiki as the platform for group collaboration, that dependence on a tech-savvy person, and thus that almost unfair balance toward the more tech-savvy person experiencing the technology goes away, because the tool is simple enough that anybody can use it. Because the tool is so intuitive and approachable, people are able to focus on the content — what they are really experts in — instead of having to spend so much time up front learning the technology.

People Are Incredible Self-Organizers

In "Why commercial wikis don't work," (Great article. Bad title. My opinion.) Chris Taylor of *Business 2.0* looked at why some highly publicized wiki experiments such as the *LA Times* Wikitorial, *A Million Penguins* book project, and Amazon's Amapedia product review wiki haven't become the major successes their creators had hoped they would be (Taylor, 2007). Taylor argues that the problem with these experiments is they rely on getting input from a community that's too large, too random, and without a common binding element. He suggests that a better way to go would be an editorial, for instance, that's edited by supporters of a particular political candidate, or a book about fishing written by fishing enthusiasts.

Despite the sensational title, the article makes a great point: Successful wiki communities need focus and a common goal to attract the right people. The idea is that a community with a common focus is more likely to produce a cohesive product that reflects that focus, because people are remarkably good at organizing themselves around a shared goal, and the flexibility of the wiki allows them to use it in a way that's best suited to their needs.

A good example of this is `Wikipatterns.com`. It exists to help anyone who's using a wiki find strategies to give their wiki the best shot at being successful. Because of that focus, it attracts people with a shared interest and gives them a place to get information — in the form of patterns to apply and anti-patterns to watch out for and fix — which they can apply to their own wiki communities. When they do so, they can come back to `Wikipatterns.com` to share what worked really well, what didn't and how they fixed it, and each time they visit the site they get more ideas. This cycle keeps building the content of the site, and enriches it with a variety of ideas and depth of knowledge that no one person could ever develop alone.

"Find Your Place in the Community"

Especially when people are first getting used to the wiki, it's important that they do it in a way that helps them see how it works, even if that means the first information they put on the wiki is something seemingly trivial such as directions for shipping a package or information about themselves in their personal profile.

People should be encouraged to find the role that best suits them, because this is an important factor in how well they engage with the wiki. A WikiChampion will be most visible early on, but new faces should become prevalent as people assume roles such as WikiGardener and PageMaintainer, and become regular contributors of content. Fixing typos, finding citations for quotes, fixing broken links, and adding links where appropriate are just as important as adding new pages and contributing content.

People who volunteer to be involved with the wiki should be especially supported because they likely have the curiosity and open-minded approach that will make them influential in building a successful collaborative community. Leaders on the wiki don't necessarily have to be the people with official titles offline, either.

For example, if one member of a team shows the most initiative and enthusiasm about the wiki, the manager of that group might designate that person the point person or PageMaintainer for wiki for that team. The point person might then be responsible for recurring activities such as posting the first version of the staff meeting agenda, reminding others to add their notes to meeting minutes, and training other team members on the wiki.

Think Process, Not Features

One of the most important differences between the traditional notion of enterprise software, and the wiki: With the wiki, it's better to think in terms of processes, not features. The traditional thinking goes something like this: When you need software to do something specific, you look for a feature that does that specific "thing," and if it's not there, you try to get the software maker to add a feature that does what you want. This takes time — often a lot of time because the software maker has to decide if it's worthwhile, add it to the software development road map, and actually develop it. It also costs more money for the software developer because it's one more thing that can add to the time required to develop a new software release, and that cost can be passed on to you in the form of higher priced software.

This is where the wiki is different. When features are added to software, they can limit how it's used because people think of the software in terms of those features. Software that's not defined by its features is more powerful because people in countless different situations can think in their specific terms about how to use it.

When people ask me about building specific features into their wikis, I explain that instead of a feature, a clever process can achieve the same goal. For example, if people need to sign off on a document that's been drafted on the wiki, they could simply add a bulleted list of the necessary reviewers right to the wiki page containing the draft document. Then each reviewer can mark their approval by putting a check next to their name or typing their initials. Presto, they've approved the content!

Because they're not signing their signatures as they would have done in the past with a paper-based system, how can their approval be verified as having come from them? It's all in the revision history! If the wiki uses standard network accounts, as would be the case in most organizations, each person's edit to mark their approval will be attributed to their username in the page's revision history.

Sometimes people need a solution and know what they need to get done, but don't know exactly how to do it in a new tool, so they think in terms of how they did it in the old tool. That's why software often starts simple and becomes increasingly complex as features are added that can constrain its use. Because the wiki is simple and flexible, it's easier to emphasize processes over features, which keeps the wiki simple, avoids that "feature creep," and ultimately makes it more useful for everyone.

Make Change the Only Constant

Introducing a wiki and shifting core activities to it offers an opportunity to examine existing processes, workflows, and ways of organizing information. Forcing people to rigidly apply existing processes to the wiki is likely to make it unsuccessful, as these ways of working may run counter to people's discovery of more efficient methods.

Encourage people to look for better ways to do things when they use the wiki, and improvements that are organically borne out of wiki use should be recognized, embraced, and rewarded. If people feel that they can have a direct impact on the way they work, and are rewarded for doing so, they'll be highly motivated to keep examining and improving their own work. Change should be the norm instead of sticking to the status quo, and anything that promotes constant smooth change will keep each team, and ultimately the whole organization, from becoming stagnant and inefficient.

Flatten Your Organization. . .in a Good Way!

When you make the cultural shift to basing information and interaction on the wiki, you can't just get work out of people and still maintain central control. When you start using a wiki, leadership has to shift to the community itself, and the structure of organizations has to evolve to become flatter so that it's easier for people all across the organization to directly work with each other. In the academic world, technology is changing the role of the teacher from a so-called "sage on the stage" to an informed guide who can help students navigate the ever-growing information in any given field. This is a reflection of the fact that one person can't possibly hold all the information and control the direction of a community. Instead the person who knows how to navigate the available resources should serve as an enabler for the things the community decides are most important. The same is true for all facets of the business world.

This doesn't mean your organization should become leaderless — it means adjusting the leadership structure to serve the community, enable it to get access to the resources it needs, and make motivated people's work easier by enabling them to get things done.

One of the best examples of an organization that's built this way is Mozilla. Its structure is open, adjustable, and highly community based. For an organization that builds open source software and relies on a distributed community of volunteer software developers around the world to build its products, its job is to provide the core services for each product community, such as coordinating the development road map for each project, maintaining the source code repositories, and planning releases, branding, and marketing. Not surprisingly, a wiki is one of Mozilla's information organization and collaboration tools: `http://wiki.mozilla.org`.

Stay Hungry. Stay Foolish.

In his 2005 Commencement address at Stanford University, Steve Jobs' parting words to the graduates were "Stay hungry. Stay foolish." They came from the final issue of *The Whole Earth Catalog*, itself a product of the collective efforts of a community, and they perfectly describe the attitude necessary to bring about change. Introducing a wiki to your organization and changing your culture for the better is an exhilarating experience. It takes time and dedication, and if you're the WikiChampion, a few odd looks the first few times you tell people about the "wiki." But it's worth it, because it creates an environment where everyone is empowered to *directly* make things happen, which gives people a deeper sense of purpose and accomplishment. It's also essential if you want to build a successful new venture, or ensure the relevance and success of an existing organization in this rapidly changing world.

References

Jobs, Steve. "Text of Steve Jobs Commencement Address (2005)," Stanford Report (14 June 2005), `http://news-service.stanford.edu/news/2005/june15/jobs-061505.html` (accessed 31 August 2007).

Taylor, Chris. "Why commercial wikis don't work," Business 2.0 (23 February 2007), `http://money.cnn.com/2007/02/21/magazines/business2/walledgardens.biz2/index.htm` (accessed 29 August 2007).

Case Study: Constitution Day

National Constitution Center — Constitution Day Website
Philadelphia Pennsylvania, USA
www.constitutioncenter.org/constitutionday
A Conversation with Tom Hillhouse, Web Services and Marketing Manager
Type of organization: Non-profit Education
Number of wiki users: 165,000 visitors/year
The National Constitution Center is an independent, non-partisan, and non-profit organization dedicated to increasing public understanding of, and appreciation for, the Constitution, its history, and its contemporary relevance, through an interactive, interpretive facility within Independence National Historical Park and a program of national outreach, so that We the People may better secure the Blessings of Liberty to ourselves and our Posterity.

The Constitution Day website serves as a directory of resources from multiple partners to help citizens celebrate Constitution Day, the birthday of our government on September 17.

1. Why did you choose a wiki?

We needed a system that would allow us to quickly publish resources to a website, and enable partners and nontechnically minded people to add and edit these resources. Essentially, we are using the wiki as a community oriented content management solution.

2.   What type of wiki are you using?

We are using a Web-based, publicly accessible website running on a commercial enterprise wiki.

3.   How are you using the wiki?

Through a permission-based wiki, a structured meta data system, and a template-based design, we are able to allow partners to add and edit their own resources as they see fit. An administrator monitors the process and makes adjustments as needed. The general public uses the website as they would any other site; they can browse, search, and download these resources.

4.   Looking at `Wikipatterns.com`, what patterns are in use on your wiki?

We use *WYSIWYG, scaffold, Overview pages, One wiki space per group,* and *Invitation.*

5.   What changes have you seen as a result of using a wiki?

We are able to distribute the tasks of maintaining content, and are able to empower users to take control of their own content.

Case Study: Peter Higgs: Using a Wiki in Research

Creative Digital Industries National Mapping Project
`http://wiki.cci.edu.au/display/NMP`

By Peter Higgs
Senior Research Fellow, Creative Digital Industries
National Mapping Project
Queensland University of Technology

I started managing a three-year research project for the ARC Centre of Excellence for Creative Industries & Innovation, a research institute within Queensland University of Technology (QUT) in mid-2004. Even though I have been involved in establishing and running with multimedia CD-ROM content production since 1992 and the internet development since 1995, I never established a website for the creative industries national mapping project: There was no point! Establishing the traditional university passive "marketing" website for the project would have required the development of an extensive brief to the "publishing" division where everything we wanted to say would have to be thought through; then there would be a series of extensive meetings, which would generate concepts and revisions. All of this would have finally lead to a static website that no one would want to visit, least of all me. Updating it would have been a similar nightmare. And none of this is a criticism of the publishing department. The procedure is perfectly appropriate for any large organization needing to communicate with 30,000 to 40,000 students and 10,000 staff.

However, the project I headed was one of about half a dozen around the world investigating definitions and statistical techniques for measuring the characteristics of what are called the creative industries. Each researcher has slightly or very different definitions, and every country has different conditions under which industrial activity and occupation statistics are classified, collected, and disseminated.

Our project was cross discipline by nature involving industry experts, economists, and statisticians with our project partners contributing to the research directly and also participating in the research steering committee. However, for the first year the collaboration aspects of the project were constrained to periodic meetings, emails and phone calls, which are very unsatisfactory as a way of harnessing group expertise and contribution capacity.

Instead I spent that year (amongst doing many other things) clarifying my requirements on ways to augment the project's capacity and influence through collaboration. I spent quite a few nights looking into various software and web based solutions that could possibly address them: FTP and webDAV servers, collaborative document websites and, through using wikipedia, with wikis appearing to be closer to what I needed. I investigated establishing a wiki using a spare Mac G4 I had at home as a server, and the only solution on paper close to meeting my requirements, which also seemed to be within reach of my limited technical skills, was Confluence. I used the experience of setting up the wiki and using it for a couple of weeks to clarify the requirements and to better express to management why a traditional website approach would be inappropriate.

It may be worth revisiting these, as they could be useful to other researchers looking to establish a wiki.

Objectives of the National Mapping Research Project Wiki

The wiki needed to provide a forum with the combination of information, participation, and functionality that will attract and retain the interest of the researchers and consultants active in the field of the creative and cultural industry mapping and economic impact research.

The wiki needed to not only publish information on the project and make available to others the resources from it, but it needed to also:

- Encourage and facilitate discussion and agreement on approaches to taxonomies and strategies.

- Provide a focused forum for the sharing of drafts, papers, reports, and statistics within the field.

- Harness the knowledge and willingness to contribute that is dispersed throughout the research and consultant community and to thereby establish a critical density of talent, effort, review, and resources.

- Allow the project's contracted participants to contribute in the day-to-day work, discussions, and decisions that interest them and at the time and place they are able to contribute.

- Substantially reduce or eliminate the frustration that project partners feel at not being up to date, not being able to participate more fully and not being able to derive the short term or even ephemeral outputs they may have a requirement for.

- Establish the CCI National Mapping Project as one of the world's pre-eminent fora in the field of creative and cultural industry mapping research.

I knew from experience that meeting these objectives would require a combination of technology capability, content that was seen as valuable, clean functional design, and an approach or aesthetic that *empowers, attracts*, and *energizes* the contributors. These last factors are very difficult to achieve and to assess in advance. By getting one of the other factors wrong, it is easy to undermine the empowerment factor so that it cannot be achieved. Furthermore, it is possible to meet the capability, content, and design requirements and still not achieve the emergence of the empowerment factor. But it needs to be strived for.

Following on from the articulation of the objectives for the project wiki, the technical requirements were established.

Sophisticated handling of Users, Groups and Access Permissions

Having spent six years managing a research project and software company in the field of rights management, I knew how critical it was to have as a foundation for the wiki a sophisticated capability of access and usage management that would require the application having an above average functionality for handling Users, Groups, and Access Permissions. It would have been a bit ambitious to hope that any existing wiki solution would also have implemented a rights expression language.

I determined that at a minimum the wiki and its supporting environment needed to be able to support at least four levels of access:

ROLE	CAPABILITY
Anonymous public	Are not able to edit pages or make comments but are able to see most of the site, as this is the only effective way of engaging new active participants.
Self-enrolled researchers and practitioners in the field	Are able to see, edit, and comment on most parts of the site. Also able to add and edit pages, resources, and forums.
Project partners, contractors, and consultants	Are able to see, edit, and comment on most parts of the site including the project administration area. Also able to add and edit pages, resources, and forums.
Project Administrator	Manage user logins, authority levels, page and global access levels.

It was likely that at least half of the users of the wiki would not be QUT staff and so the use of QUT LDAP connected authentication system was problematic. It was neither feasible nor desirable to provide QUT access accounts to all possible project contributors or even a select number of them. And to require a formal approach of "please request an account and we will issue you one in a couple of days" would reduce the number of people able to engage with the project.

All aspects of the wiki had to facilitate the stages of project engagement. The wiki was seen to be a critical method with which to establish virtuous cycles, which would lead to it becoming a viable dynamic community. The wiki needed to support the natural stages that people go through when they engage with a community, project, or product.

STAGE	DESCRIPTION
Attraction	The wiki needed to be "infectious"; it needed to support Google and other site ranking services to ensure that the wiki has prominence when relevant criteria are searched for. It needed to support short and human readable URLs to its pages unlike content management systems.
Interest	Once the site is reached, the "seeker" needed to be encouraged to stay and explore more.

STAGE	DESCRIPTION
Desire	The wiki needed to be engaging so the seeker explores more deeply into the structure of the site and develops a strong commitment to the idea that the wiki can provide meaningful solutions to the seeker's needs.
Action	The wiki needed to encourage the seeker to engage, commit, and contribute to the content on the site.
Retention	The wiki needed to be "sticky." It needed to provide real, social, and psychological benefits to return to the wiki often, to participate, contribute, and possible integrate into their day-to-day workflow.
Expansion	The wiki needed to be "infectious"; it needed to encourage and support the existing participants to bring in and engage other researchers and contributors who can enrich the project.

Collaboration

The wiki needed to encourage and facilitate true multidirectional collaboration in a number of ways:

- Editing (with version histories) of pages
- Comments and threads
- Adding of sections, pages, resources, and attachments
- Addition of other spaces for other projects, which may be highly similar or in a related field
- Federation with other projects through RSS and cross-linking

Ease of Use: The Thin End of the Wedge

I knew from experience that the emotive appeal and the ease of use of the wiki would be critical to the success of the project. The usability of the wiki had to be such that anyone can feel at ease contributing without them thinking they are damaging the system or even worse, thinking they have to be HTML coders. It was essential that the wiki was not technically daunting or did not block novice users from making their first, simple contribution of perhaps making a comment, fixing a typo, or correcting a definition.

With each contribution they make they gain more confidence and might start to explore how to make their posting look as good as some of the others through, say, bullet points or table formatting.

Addressing the "Why Nots?"

Of course getting any new approach approved is rather interesting and there were the normal questions such as, "Well, why not just use the corporate website?" That was pretty easy to address. The next question, obviously from the IT department was, "Well, we already have a content management system, why not use it?"

"Why Not Use Our Existing Content Management System?"

A competent wiki will almost certainly include a content management system layer but the users will never see it or be aware of it. I know of no existing CMS that has built in the functionality needed for a wiki. And even if it did chances are that it would be unsuited for tailoring to meet the requirements of a wiki, especially that of the ease of use. It is the psychology of the tool that is critical: CMSs are used, configured, and controlled by technologists to support their objectives. Wikis on the other hand are tools focused on the needs of end users and should require even less technical sophistication than using a word processor. It would take an exceptional amount of work to make a CMS into a competent wiki.

Getting It Accepted into a Corporate Environment

We obtained approval to move the prototype I was running at home onto a linux server within the Creative Industries faculty with a 50-user license from Atlassian. Within a couple of months there were three or four additional spaces on the server for other projects within Creative Industries. The NMP space increased to about 120 pages pretty quickly and the management team started to use it and refer to it.

Word spread, the QUT IT department obtained an enterprise license of Confluence and JIRA for them to use internally with a view to at some stage rolling it out for teaching and learning.

How Are We Using the Wiki?

The wiki has been in use within QUT now for just over a year and is essentially still in the first generation of usage being fairly straightforward: The site has areas on the project background, objectives, and findings. A resources area includes links to reports and other projects. There are lots of tables and links.

But the real expansion in the usage of the NMP wiki has come from its flexibility and availability to be used for projects that have a high coordination requirement within a relatively short time frame. Putting together tenders and proposals for research consortia has grown the number of spaces on the server to almost 20 with the number of registered users approaching 200. In more traditional uses aside from projects, PhD candidates have established spaces as semiprivate blogs that are narratives of their research journey.

We haven't yet connected the wiki to an external database for more sophisticated reference book management, nor has it been integrated with the LDAP server for authentication. But these will happen soon.

The server is managed (when required) by a QUT IT specialist who uploads and configures the server and any updates. No other technical assistance has been sought to date, so augmentation has occurred only when the nontechnical manager (myself) could find a solution to a pressing need. So the addition of macros and other plug-ins has been relatively slow as there has not been enough free time to evaluate and test them. We have implemented a couple such as the repository plug-in (amazing!) and the formatting plug-ins. Being able to read Excel and Word files has made it much easier to post content, especially formatted spreadsheets, directly in a page.

The Wiki as eResearch Infrastructure

The second generation of usage we envisage as using Confluence as the foundation or infrastructure for delivering a number of eResearch services that are currently too technically challenging for the nontechnical researchers or too specific a requirement for a smallish group to be justified supporting.

QUT's ARC Centre of Excellence for Creative Industries & Innovation is conducting a significant range of research over the next five years into the nature of creative industries and creative innovation, social networks, the cluster effects, and the creation and evolution of participatory media. To conduct meaningful research often requires sophisticated web-based systems where the behaviors and responses can be established and observed. But as budgets are tight, it is important to be able to share and re-use not just the technical code components, but also the processes and procedures.

One way to achieve this is to use Confluence as a foundation service and source or develop the other functionality required on top of Confluence including new interface metaphors without detracting from its basic wiki appeal.

Research Publications, Reference, and Citation Management

University research is changing in many disciplines, including creative industries. Subject matter is getting more and more complex, and published material is doubling every few years. Managing your sources, key points, prioritizing and grouping references and citations used to be just hard. But with multi-discipline teams becoming more the norm, how does a team of researchers communicate, share, and efficiently manage their research source material; with both original material and that from others, how do they share and preserve a link to the things they think are excellent, insightful, or just well phrased and which might be useful, if not this week, next month, or even next year. Online services such as CiteULike.com and delicious, and applications such as Adobe Acrobat's catalog function, EndNote, and DevonThink Professional (for Mac users) can help, but they don't really get to the heart of a networked, group-based research material resource.

The existing electronic holdings within a department of reports such as journals, articles, case studies, and books could have their meta data entered into the register either manually or through pulling in references via DOIs, citation links, or ISBNs. The NMP project has a relatively large holding of some 1,000 or so government reports that are not on standard citation systems, and these would have to be entered manually.

Why is this important? To facilitate the searching and browsing of relevant research within a domain and most importantly to aid the researcher community to accrete over time its knowledge and its knowledge of the knowledge.

Researchers within a field would be encouraged to register their own reports into a structure database with a simple forms front end, which would include links to the download of electronic copies.

Additional functionality would allow electronic copies of reports that are held on internal repositories to be available online to authorized users. They can access the report and add layers of additional information such as document pages and paragraph level tags (folksonomy), and allow a section or paragraph of the native document such as PDF or Word to be marked up for extraction, commented on, and automatically resaved onto the server.

Authorized users could then search for the specific tags and harvest the relevant marked-up extracts and their references, perhaps store them in databases, and then collate them into a report with citation management. Ideally this usage is then reflected back into the research archive so that you can keep track of what has been quoted.

The closest I have been able to identify is the NeuroScholar system at `http://sourceforge.net/projects/neuroscholar/` which is obviously optimized to the requirements of neurology research. It would be excellent to be able to adapt the NeuroScholar source code that is available under an LGPL to the more general research document requirements and to put it onto Confluence.

Project and Team Management

Confluence currently supports dynamic task lists, but research always requires more sophisticated project planning, team, and task management. At the simplest putting a project proposal together with short deadlines requires online project management, task delegation, collation, and reporting. And very often this has to happen in the midst of very full calendar.

The NMP project is looking for an online project management service similar to that currently offered by BaseCampHQ but on top of Confluence to facilitate the establishment and planning of projects and the tracking of tasks, people, and resources.

It is possible that Atlassian could be the best organization to provide this by re-skinning a subset of JIRA, Atlassian's bug and feature management tool that is the sister application to the Confluence wiki.

Network Enhancers: People, Organizations, and Projects

The ARC Centre of Excellence for Creative Industries & Innovation (CCI) at Queensland University of Technology currently has a number of research projects that require it to either establish forums for the creation and exchange of new and existing digital content or to facilitate the growth of communities of practice such as the networks between small firms and sole practitioners of different creative disciplines that could team up for a short-term project.

CCI believes the answer to better understanding the dynamics of Creative Industry clusters may lie in providing Web 2.0 petri dishes: *networking sandboxes* or a *linkage enhancer*, which combine the functionality of a growth medium and also provide a rich source of anonymized or pseudo-anonymized data of the interactions for research analysis. It has proposed the development of a hybrid system built on top of Confluence that is part research infrastructure, part linkage conduit, and part team management.

For individuals and companies within a community or discipline members, the linkage enhancer would act similarly to LinkedIn.com or Orkut.com with ways to discover and maintain links with people with specific talents, products, and projects in a specific domain.

Communication within the community would be facilitated through an escalation of online forums such as the traditional functions of a wiki: newsgroups, blogs, newsletters, chat, and email.

Linkages between individuals and the companies they have worked with or the projects they worked on would be maintained by using more structured data handled by the system (similarly to LinkedIn.com and Orkut.com) but once a profile has been established, actions provide the data necessary for keeping the profiles up to date.

For firms or individuals wishing to locate a person or company with a specific skill or history of working on a project then this can be discovered through the directories built into the system.

Where a team is formed either to develop a proposal or to execute a project, the management of the team, the milestones and tasks and the communications within the team would be facilitated by the online system. In this respect the

Linkage enhancer would have similar functionality to a lightweight version of `Groove.net` groupware.

All the time the system is managing the tracking and reporting of the activities and interactions on a number of levels — some anonymous, some pseudo-anonymous, and some fully identified according to system, research, and user preferences.

In this way the system would update profiles with project and participation details that are suitable for publication to the public, to peers and prospects. Research on the network effects and the growth in interaction activity can be conducted from the wealth of data that would be captured.

The deployment of the Linkage enhancer would be via local industry groups and associations hopefully with the support of local and state government. If as envisaged, the system is truly distributed, then those groups wishing to provide a customized and special focus enhancer could do so without reducing the effectiveness of the linkages and network building with other disciplines and regions.

Handling, Presenting, and Commenting on Structured Data

The majority of research requires the development and use of specific terms, most often terms that are part of structured hierarchical category or classification schemes.

Developing an accurate scheme is critical for segment analysis purposes as:

- It is very difficult to capture, store, or perform statistical analysis on measurements of things that cannot consistently be described. This enables use.

- Measurements of things are only useful to other parties if the other parties know what has been measured and how it has been measured in order to permit these measures to correspond to their own approach. This requires comparable units of measurement for the objects that have been described in common. This enables re-use.

A well-structured category scheme enables the patterns and the relationships buried in diverse and large populations and collections to be seen.

Classification Registries/Commentaries

To fulfill its objectives the National Mapping Project has established databases containing the hierarchical records of existing standard classifications for industry of employment, occupation of employment, and qualifications. These are all then mapped to an abstract classification spine to allow a more unified view and their consistent use in analytical programs.

It is difficult to communicate these cascades, as there are many levels and many dimensions.

Outliners such as those supported by the OPML project allows a pagetree-like view of a single classification structure. But Confluence does not currently support the display of OPML files from its content plug-in, so we are currently working to develop such a plug-in. Even when this is available it will still be difficult for another research to comment on a specific point in a cascade or to suggest an alternative.

Visualizing the links between different releases of a classification or between different types of classification is difficult using drawing programs and near to impossible any other way currently. Integrating and optimizing the functionality of something like the Hypergraph plug-in, which uses the GraphXML with an OPML XML or a direct link to an XML-based classification registry service could also be an approach.

Conclusions

The experience of the last year in implementing and expanding the use of Confluence has left no doubt to the substantial benefits of a well-engineered enterprise wiki over using a traditional web server approach. Even at its most basic level of implementation and usage, Confluence allows researchers to take direct control of the publishing and communication with their collaborators and community with a minimum of distraction.

The full potential of the wiki approach will begin to be realized when the things that previously required dedicated sophisticated application to achieve can be delivered simply and effectively by adding functionality onto Confluence. Extending the functionality through utilizing common resources, attracting a higher proportion of the interaction from a growing proportion of a research community and facilitating this in a federated seamless manner will generate substantial positive network effects. One mechanism to accelerate the research community's adoption of Confluence and other advanced wikis would be to establish focused online communities to discuss the usage and possible research specific enhancements. This should also include opt-in listings of those wikis used for research along with case studies of the impact of the wiki on the research.

Questions & Answers

When people are thinking about how they might use a wiki, they'll have a lot of questions about basic editing issues, privacy of information, how the wiki works in relation to email and other tools, and how to get started. Answering these questions is key to getting to that all-important first edit — the moment when they actually start using the wiki. Here are some questions I've been asked at various workshops, conferences, and by people whose wiki adoption I've advised.

Someone else can change what I wrote?

Yes. The basic function of a wiki is to enable people to collaboratively create and edit content using a website that can be easily edited using just a web browser. Within an organization's wiki, who can see and change what you've written is determined by who has access to the same wiki space as you, which is often just the people working on the same team or project as you.

Although it can seem disconcerting at first, this is what makes wiki collaboration so powerful. The technical ability to easily make changes to what someone else has written raises the personal and social responsibility to make those changes in a way that respects what others have done. Therefore, when someone makes a change to something you've written, it's incumbent upon them to do things like leaving a comment about the changes they've made (this is good practice especially with regard to significant changes), and making their changes in a way that builds on the best of what others have contributed.

When someone else edits a page, how do I see what changes they made?

Whenever changes are made to a wiki page, the wiki stores a record of those changes in its revision history, so you can see exactly what was added, changed, or deleted each time a page is edited. The revision history is an important window into the content that you see on the "surface" of a wiki page, because it shows how that page arrived at the current version you see today.

For example, let's take two people collaborating by emailing a Word document back and forth and making changes. Each time one person makes changes, whatever they delete or edit in the document is lost as soon as they save their changes, and the only way to look at earlier versions is to search through the chain of email for an older version of the document. Even then, you'd have to manually compare the two documents to see changes.

The wiki simplifies this significantly by keeping the document and its revision history together in one place. When you compare revisions it highlights the changes, typically marking additions in green and deletions in red. The revision history also allows changes to be easily reverted if necessary. For example, if content was mistakenly deleted from the page, an earlier version of the page could be restored from the revision history in a matter of seconds.

Can the wiki notify me when a page is changed?

You can monitor changes to a page by email or RSS feed. Once you've elected to "watch" a page, you'll receive an email or new item in your RSS feed when the page has been changed. This is especially useful if you want to keep up with a number of wiki pages and don't have time to manually check each one. Notification also helps maintain a healthy level of activity on wiki pages because the notification helps people stay aware of what's happening on the wiki, and they're more likely to actively contribute when they're engaged with what's happening on an ongoing basis.

What if I don't like what someone else wrote? Can I just delete it?

It's better to change than just delete. If you're going to make major changes, you might ask your team or community for consensus first. In addition to directly editing the content of a page, wikis provide space to comment, and this is the ideal place to discuss potential changes or deletions to a page's content.

Discussing changes, especially if they're likely to have a significant impact on the content of a page, is a good way to avoid becoming known as a *Do-it-all* — someone who overpowers the collaborative nature of the wiki by taking it upon themselves to make unilateral changes.

What if someone puts a contribution into a wiki page, and then somebody else just deletes it, puts something completely different in, another person just deletes that, and puts yet another different contribution in. Doesn't there still have to be some moderator?

This is very unlikely to happen. Good practice on a wiki discourages simply deleting someone else's work, and in practice people are much more likely to do just the opposite — they'll add their own contribution and won't even touch what someone else has written. This most often happens with new users who are afraid to change what someone else has written. The best thing one person can do is make contributions that build on the existing content.

Let's say you add a new wiki page and post a draft news release. I edit it to add a new sentence at the end of the fourth paragraph. When I click Save, the current version of the page is going to have my new sentence added to that paragraph. When you visit the page, you might check the revision history to get a quick overview of my changes to the page and see the new sentence. You might decide that my new sentence belongs in the middle of the paragraph and should be combined with another, so you move it and edit those two together.

Once you click Save, your revisions then become the new current version of the page. After you save the page, you might leave a comment explaining the rationale for your changes, and the next time I look at the page, I can see both your changes and your reasoning for making them. This way, we can work at times that are most convenient, and not necessarily have to be in direct contact to discuss changes.

So what you have with a wiki is not one person who is entirely charged with dealing with all of that change, but shared responsibility among all collaborators to make their changes integrate with what others have contributed, use the best of other contributions, and take an approach that emphasizes refining content.

If the debate on a wiki page does get "hot," can you somehow shut off editing?

Enterprise wiki software lets you set permissions for reading and editing pages, so you can turn privileges on and off as needed. It's important to note that the instances you've probably heard about regarding situations on Wikipedia where editing has been shut off for a period of time — a cooling-off period if the debate gets to be really hot — are specific to the type of community on Wikipedia. That scenario doesn't happen in organizations because when people are working toward a shared goal, they don't get into the type of heated exchanges that happen in open, anonymous, all-virtual communities.

In organizations, editing and discussion on pages will ebb and flow naturally at certain points. For instance, if people are working on a document, report, or project and there's a deadline, they'll finalize their editing as they reach the deadline. After that deadline, the pace of editing may pick up again when changes need to be made.

Can *everyone* see what I put on the wiki? What if some material is sensitive or confidential?

Enterprise wikis allow you to easily create multiple wiki spaces for different groups, teams, and projects, and give people appropriate access to read and edit pages. Using these permissions, groups can collaborate privately when necessary, and work across boundaries when necessary.

For example, your team can have a wiki space where the ability to view and edit pages is restricted to just members of your team, but if you're working with someone in another team, you can give them access to view or edit certain pages in your wiki.

How do I give people access to it/restrict access?

Wiki a wiki, you don't have to ask the system administrator or IT staff to do this — you can do it yourself. For example, in Confluence you can set the permissions for any page directly from the page itself. When you're in edit mode, the option to give individual users or groups of people read or edit access is just below the content editing area.

Keep in mind that restricting access should be done carefully, and really only when it's necessary to safeguard a particular page with sensitive data. Otherwise, it's best to keep the wiki as open as possible to encourage people to share their information and be transparent.

How can I control the wiki and approve edits?

There's a fine line between using permissions to manage access to wiki spaces and controlling the wiki itself. Wiki is successful where knowledge management and content management tools have failed because it allows you to strike a balance between control and creative, organic growth.

If there's no restriction at all, the tool may be less successful because people need some guidance on how to use it and knowledge that it's secure before trusting it with sensitive information. On the flip side, too much control restricts people from fully participating because if it's presented with narrow restrictions on its use, they will be less likely to experiment with different ways of using it.

How do I know the content on the wiki is correct?

This question is an extension of the oft asked, "How do I know the content on Wikipedia is correct?" and it subtly assumes that the information is probably not correct. If you use a wiki in your organization, and it mimics the existing social and organizational structure by being used within existing teams and projects, the information it contains will be as correct as any other information source, such as email, PDF or Word documents, or paper documents.

Furthermore, if you find something in the wiki to be incorrect, you can fix it immediately, and it will be fixed for everyone who uses that information. In a comparative sense, that makes the wiki capable of being more correct than other sources of information.

Is there a grammarian or controller?

A wiki isn't just controlled by one person; the community collectively maintains the quality and growth of content. Some common roles are self-identified by various members of a wiki community. For example, a *WikiGnome*, also known as a *WikiGardener*, is someone who devotes time to maintaining the site, organizing pages, ensuring that links work, and improving the flow and clarity of content. A WikiGardener sets an excellent example for productive behaviors and contribution to the wiki's value.

A passionate, enthusiastic *WikiChampion* is essential to the success of wiki because she or he can generate interest, give the appropriate amount of training for each person at the right time, monitor growth of the tool, and fix problems that could derail adoption.

In some instances, a team might make use of the *PageMaintainer* role to coordinate activity. Although this role might sound closest to some sort of controller, the PageMaintainer's job primarily has to do with the activity surrounding content, not the content itself. For example, the PageMaintainer might be responsible to encourage input, make sure others have added their contributions to a meeting agenda, minutes, or action item checklist, and maintain the organization of pages for tracking team meetings.

So what should I do first?

A good strategy for a person's first contact with a wiki is an *Invitation* to create a profile, like *MySpace*. For one thing, it's useful to have standard information about people, like phone numbers, email addresses, IM screen names, and website URLs in an easy-to-access *and easy-to-update* place.

It's the difficulty of updating that hinders most other types of content management and website creation tools, but this isn't the case with wiki so it's a much more attractive option. Personal pages also give people a place to write about themselves and the ease of doing this can make the first experience using a wiki enjoyable.

Building pages is also good for building community because people can help each other with questions or problems. Even just informally discussing things like what to include on the pages gets people talking about a common thread, and it doesn't have the same formality as working on a project.

What would I put on the wiki?

This depends on your purpose for using the wiki. The best uses of the wiki are those that are highly focused on solving a particular problem — updating documentation, simplifying project management, keeping track of constantly changing information that needs to be updated by a team, and so on. Therefore, the best way to decide what to put on the wiki is to look at your day-to-day work processes and see what can benefit from being put on the wiki.

One example I regularly give to groups and teams looking for where to start is to put meeting agendas on the wiki, then have team members record minutes during and after meetings, and use the wiki to track action items and projects. This way it's easy to know exactly where everything stands at any given time, and by starting your wiki use at the core of the team's interaction, it will become indispensable for obvious things like collaboration and project management, and new uses will spring up as people interact with it.

Can it handle images and other file types?

Yes. Images can be inserted inline with the text on a wiki page, so they appear in appropriate places throughout the content. Although text is the core of a wiki, visual elements such as images, diagrams, and video can be essential parts of the content, and can be included on wiki pages. In fact, video sites such as YouTube, Brightcove, and Google Video have made it very easy to embed video on pages because they host the content and you just place a small snippet of code where you want the video to appear on the wiki page.

Also, you can attach files to wiki pages so that all the information pertaining to a topic can be easily kept in one place. For example, a wiki page for a meeting could contain the agenda and minutes, and also have files related to topics discussed or slides from a presentation attached to it. By doing this, everything related to that meeting is organized in one place and can be found on a moment's notice.

Can I get content out of the wiki, say, when I'm done drafting a document?

Because the content you are putting in a Wiki is simply text, getting it out can be as simple as copying and pasting. Although in most cases you probably wouldn't do this, it's nice to know that you're not dealing with proprietary file formats when you use a wiki.

When you need the contents of a wiki page in a more traditional format, it's possible to export a wiki page into a Word document or PDF file. When you export a wiki page, the wiki will automatically convert any wiki markup items, such as bold or italicized text and hyperlinks into the formatting used in the file format to which you export.

How do I get people to switch from email to use the wiki?

You don't have to completely drop email; it's better to use wiki for content, and then send email linking to wiki page at first. This directs people to the wiki, and makes it less of a dramatic transition. Over time people will get used to going directly to the wiki.

Also, the wiki can email you when pages are changed, so email is still useful in the wiki world. Now it's just put to better use because it does what it does best — communicates what's happening in the wiki, which helps encourage collaboration on the wiki.

Is it ok to work locally, (i.e. offline on my own computer) on content that will go in the wiki?

Sure. Some people will start writing some content locally on their own computer, and then add it to the wiki page when they're ready. Typically when people are making a quick change or a quick addition to a page, they'll just do that right on the wiki, but if you're traveling or in some situation where you don't have Internet access, it's fine to work on some content locally, and then transfer it to the wiki. I do this especially when I'm flying — I'll write draft blog posts while I'm in the air, and then add them to a wiki page, which is my staging area for posts to be published.

What if you read what someone wrote on a wiki page and find a grammatical error or can't tell what the person wants to say?

If you find a minor grammatical error, I'd just edit the page and fix it. If there's something you really don't understand, you can comment on the page to point out the ambiguity and ask for clarification. Even in this case, I'd try to edit the page and refine what the other person wrote. That way, next time they look at the wiki they'll see that I've made changes and can look at how I've revised the original wording. Whether it's now really far off from what they originally meant, or closer to their intended message, they can revise it further if necessary.

What this example illustrates is the change in thinking between the way we've done it before and the way we do it with a wiki, because in the way we've done it before you don't make immediate changes to things. You often find a change and you tell somebody else, "Here's a change that you might want to make." On a wiki, you just make the change right there. To a certain extent you're making a change for that person, but in a community where people are actively working on this, people begin to learn from each other's work.

So if you go in and you write something, and I go in and refine it, and you like what I have written better than the original, you might then adjust your writing style a little bit. These things happen gradually over time. And because of the ability to work so directly with something, those changes happen in a much more fluid way.

What would motivate someone to contribute to a wiki? Seems like they get less credit than they'd get for sending an email, where everyone sees they sent it?

Actually, in my experience email isn't the best way to get noticed for your good ideas. Most people get so much email they they're in a very defensive mode when they deal with their inboxes, that is they want to whittle the number down to just what they have to directly answer and ignore the rest. Also, when they see too many emails from one person that just go to a large list of recipients, they're likely to just consider the them annoying and bordering on spam.

When a team uses a wiki, people go to it with a very different mindset. It doesn't feel nearly as overwhelming as email because people don't have to deal with an overload of messages where every one (that's not junk) needs a response directly from them. On the wiki, they can edit the page to add contributions where they feel they're most relevant. Also, if they read something they really like, they can see who added it, and are more likely to do so when they're intrinsically motivated to find out about something they like.

In a small, known audience, your reputation becomes tied to what you contribute, which motivates people to add the kind of valuable content that keeps building their reputation among the people with whom they work closely.

What would you say is the biggest difference between the wiki and content management systems when used for project management?

With a wiki, the single biggest difference is that content is put in the wiki during the project, not after the fact. This switch takes a little time to happen, but once it does, people see the wiki as the active hub for the project, not just a passive "file cabinet" in which to dump everything after a project is finished.

In the long term, this is really important because it gets people in the mindset that creating knowledge related to projects is a dynamic process, which makes revising and evolving the project much easier.

Isn't this just another enterprise IT project with a lot of promise but little chance of success?

If you think of it as the be-all-and-end-all solution to everything that's not working in your organization, then yes. Anytime the technology is hyped as opposed to focusing on solving problems with collaboration, knowledge organization, it inevitably becomes a disappointment because it can't live up to such high levels of hype.

It's better to look at what's not working as efficiently as possible, and emphasize solving the problem. People respond better to a "let's figure out the best way to solve this" approach than the "this tool will solve your problems so you must use it" approach (that's what we all don't like about the stereotypical sales pitch).

So how about measuring the ROI of so called "Enterprise 2.0" tools like the wiki?

Right now, I don't think you can define wiki/Enterprise 2.0 success based on return on investment. Many reasons for this are: most Enterprise 2.0 tools cost pennies compared to their more expensive 1.0 brethren. Second, how you measure productivity from Enterprise 2.0 tools will vary considerably from one application or one knowledge worker to another. Lastly, and this may sound naive, but the rapid popularity of Enterprise 2.0 tools tells me that these applications have filled a niche that the market was craving for a long time. They have succeeded because they fill a niche that traditional Office and 1.0 applications didn't work for. As a result, some 1.0 tools are falling by the wayside as outmoded and outdated technology. By contrast, 2.0 tools have offered immediate gratification, which is a subtle form of ROI. Blogs are a good example of an application that has offered immediate gratification to millions of people who were craving a new means of communication. Wikis have given instant gratification to teams that have long needed a simple, easy-to-use and truly useful collaboration and knowledge construction platform. The more these tools become enmeshed in the landscape of organizations, the more likely you can call them a success. Time will tell.

What about IT? Won't they say "No" to adding yet another tool they have to support?

Chances are, they already use a wiki. Because of its origin as a tool created by software developers and others in the technology world to track projects and document software code and design patterns, a wiki is often already present somewhere within IT departments.

If this is the case, the trick is to develop a strategy for growing wiki use outside IT (as well as inside too — there are probably plenty of people even within an IT department that haven't had much exposure to the wiki.)

The best strategy is to conduct a pilot with a carefully selected group. This keeps growth in check and allows you to demonstrate the value of broader wiki use, work out any kinks, and develop standard procedures for account and space creation, new user induction, and support.

How do I convince others to use the wiki?

It's best not to push people too hard, lest they push back and resist using the wiki. Having said that, the best way to help someone see the value of the wiki is to show examples. Tell stories that are supported by examples from your pilot. Show people how others in similar situations have been able to solve a problem or improve how they work.

Often people just need to see an example of success to feel more confident about trying something new, and if they can talk to others who have directly benefited from using the wiki, they'll get a chance to have their questions answered and their skepticism about something new and unfamiliar reduced. Also, as they hear the specifics of others' use, they can relate it to their own needs and begin to formulate a concrete plan for their own wiki use.

What's the advantage of constructing knowledge on a wiki?

When a group collaboratively builds knowledge on a wiki, the wiki captures not just the knowledge itself, but the context in which the knowledge is produced. The ability to post comments on pages alongside the content lets people discuss changes, post notes about their edits, and document the growth of content in a way that helps other collaborators make meaningful contributions. The revision history also adds context to the knowledge because it reveals the process by which it's constructed, and shows the personal and social factors and biases that influence peoples' contributions.

For me, this is one of the realizations that came out of the Wikipedia-Britannica controversy stemming from *Nature*'s comparison of the two (for more on this, see Chapter 2). The Britannica editors claimed that the knowledge in their encyclopedia is of high quality because a group of experts decide what to include, but there's no way for the average reader to verify this. On Wikipedia, anyone can look at the revision history for any page, and see the history of that page from the first edit to the present. Being able to see that gives a person the ability to see into the content they're consuming on the site, and make a more informed decision about it's comprehensiveness and accuracy. It also empowers people to help make the content more neutral and accurate if they find something is missing or the content is biased.

But this is all still quite new. When they find an error, some people still just leave a comment instead of just editing the page and fixing it. That's because it takes time for the shift to take hold, and for people to realize that they have much more direct power to improve the content, and that the proverbial "someone else" who used to fix things is now them.

How do you encourage context-building and conversation about the changes that occur on the wiki?

For instance, when you edit a wiki page, it's a really good idea to leave a brief comment explaining your edits. This allows others to see why you made a change, which is especially helpful in a community where people don't always have the opportunity to meet physically (such as when people are in offices in different cities or countries).

Also, have a look at the revision history and previous comments before you edit. This can help you put your edits in context and make sure you don't inadvertently step on someone's toes by practically reverting a previous change. How you acknowledge others, and their edits, ultimately affects how they, in turn, acknowledge you and your contributions.

If you feel the need to make a significant change, such as deleting some content from a page, don't just do it immediately. Instead, post a comment indicating that you want to make the change, and asking for opinions and feedback on the proposed changes. This does two things. First, it informs people about a change so that if they read the page after you've made that change, they can see why material was significantly altered or removed. Second, it gives people a chance to voice their own opinions about the proposed changes, and reduces the chance that people have a dispute over changes to a page. People are most likely to react negatively when they feel they've been left out of a change, or haven't had a chance to voice their opinions. If you give them a chance to do so before the change is made, you may get some excellent feedback that makes for better changes in the long run, and builds a stronger sense of community and dialogue around changes.

Can using a wiki help make conversations and collaboration more inclusive, especially of those who are more reluctant to speak up in a face-to-face meeting?

I think that, when used as a complement to the face-to-face activities of a group, the wiki adds another dimension to the ways people can share their ideas, opinions, and contributions. Some people are less comfortable sharing their opinions in person, and are more likely to share them online, when they have more time to articulate their points, and are less pressured to immediately offer follow-up comments or rebuttal to differing opinions. For instance, if someone offers an idea on the wiki, and someone else posts a comment asking for further details, clarification on a specific point, or simply offers a differing opinion, the author of the original idea can reflect on the comments and take time to craft a well thought out reply.

Also, use of the wiki can provide a space for discussions and collaboration to continue after a face-to-face meeting has ended, or before one has started. In the former case, this allows people to keep working on an issue in a way that fits their schedules and allows each to contribute when it's most convenient. In the latter case, starting discussion and collaboration on a topic can make the in-person meeting much more productive because people will already have begun work and identified the areas that need further discussion during the meeting. This results in shorter, more focused meetings, and the cycle of online and in-person collaboration takes advantage of the best of both, and makes the process more inclusive of everyone involved.

Index

Index